BLACK RACIAL ATTITUDES

Trends and Complexities

howard schuman
shirley hatchett

Survey Research Center ● Institute for Social Research
The University of Michigan
Ann Arbor, Michigan
1974

ISR Code No. 3589

E185.615
S29

Library of Congress Catalog Card No. 74-620067
ISBN 0-87944-157-7 paperbound
ISBN 0-87944-158-5 clothbound

Published by the Institute for Social Research
The University of Michigan, Ann Arbor, Michigan 48106

PREFACE

Gunnar Myrdal, in his introduction to *An American Dilemma*, states that the racial problem in the United States is fundamentally "a white man's problem." The important fact, he argues, is "that practically all the economic, social, and political power is held by whites," and therefore it is necessary "to give *primary* attention to what goes on in the minds of white Americans" (1964, p. lxxv). In line with these assumptions, most enlightened writing since Myrdal's time has focused on white attitudes and beliefs, and more recently on white-controlled institutional structures.

Without denying Myrdal's main premise, the present monograph clearly does not accept his conclusion completely.[1] From the standpoint of both race relations and the larger fate of American society, we believe black attitudes, beliefs, and actions are of considerable importance, and deserve the same descriptive and analytic attention as do those of whites. Constituting more than a tenth of the American population, and from a quarter to over half the population in many major cities, blacks are not without economic, political, or moral force in America. Their strategic location in the United States, along with the importance of color as a world-wide issue, gives them a significance even beyond their considerable numbers. In the final analysis blacks may be subject to white power, but it is also true that the future of American society for both blacks and whites is inextricably tied to the resolution of our racial problems, and that in this sphere blacks are an active and potent force.

Furthermore, the slogan "study the victimizers, not the victims" can too easily become an excuse for substituting the ideologies and preconceptions of white and black intellectuals for the often different reality revealed by empirical research. In this monograph we have tried to present a modest but complex set of data gathered using attitude sample survey methods, and to do so within a relatively objective framework of analysis and reporting. We do not doubt that our own values have influenced the investigation in many respects, nor have we sought to avoid every phrase of

---

[1]Fortunately, Myrdal did not restrict himself to his own framework. *An American Dilemma* is particularly rich in its discussion of black social structure, culture, and attitudes.

MAR 21 1980

interpretation which represents these values. But we have tried to stay close to what is perhaps the most essential strength of social scientific method: the capacity to disconfirm one's own hypotheses and wishes. We know this has happened at points, for some of our results were neither expected nor desired.

Of course, we do not assume that the approach through attitude surveys is the only useful one. In this area, even more than in some others, there is need for a variety of empirical investigations, from participant-observation on the one side (see Hannerz, 1969) to analysis of demographic and socio-economic data on the other (see Duncan, 1967). The attitude survey is simply one, and not the least useful, of several approaches.

*   *   *   *

The present report draws on three separate sample surveys, and therefore on the thought and work of a great many people.

1. The 1968 survey for the National Advisory Commission on Civil Disorders was carried out in collaboration with Angus Campbell, and the joint report on "Racial Attitudes in Fifteen American Cities" by Campbell and Schuman (1968) constituted in many ways the starting point for the present investigation. Data collection for that survey was supported by the Ford Foundation, and subsequent analysis by a grant to Angus Campbell from the National Institute for Mental Health (MH 18101-02).

2. The second data set essential for our time comparisons comes from the 1968 Detroit Area Study, which Howard Schuman carried out in collaboration with Jean M. Converse and James S. House. That survey, and an important part of the analysis for this report, were greatly aided by a grant to Schuman from the National Institute for Mental Health (MH 15537-02).

3. The collection of the 1971 data on black attitudes, which allows our most important time comparison, was made possible by Schuman's work with Otis Dudley Duncan on a larger Detroit Area Study of social change, supported by the Russell Sage Foundation. Shirley Hatchett, a graduate student in the Detroit Area Study in 1971, played a key role in seeing that black attitudes were part of that replication, and subsequently worked on the analysis and writing for this monograph.

Many other persons shared significantly in designing and carrying through the three surveys drawn on here. Their advice and help are acknowledged in several of the publications listed in the Bibliography, particularly in Campbell and Schuman (1968) and Duncan, Schuman, and Duncan (1973).

Otis Dudley Duncan provided a number of valuable suggestions on an earlier draft of the first five chapters of this monograph. A penultimate draft of the complete monograph was read by Willard Rodgers, and we are grateful to him for several very useful additions. As will be obvious, neither Professor Duncan nor Dr. Rodgers is responsible for remaining sins of omission or commission.

It is pleasant to acknowledge the assistance of Peg Bertsch in moving this volume from very rough penned drafts to final typescript; her cooperation, skill, and judgment have been a genuine asset. Lee Behnke prepared the graphs presented herein. William Haney encouraged our enterprise from the start, and we have gained from his editorial judgment at many points along the way.

CONTENTS

TABLES

FIGURES

1

BLACK ATTITUDES
AT THREE POINTS IN TIME

The early months of 1968 were a period of primary attention to urban racial problems in America. The major riots in Detroit, Newark, and other cities had occurred just a few months earlier. A Presidential Commission was working intensively on a report, to be issued in March 1968, dealing with the causes and prevention of "civil disorders"—a euphemism for black riots, or uprisings, or rebellions—what they were to be called was itself at issue. In April of 1968, Martin Luther King was assassinated by a white man, and the death of this nonviolent activist precipitated violence in a new set of cities (including the nation's capital) which had largely escaped previous rioting. Two of the surveys discussed here took place in this crowded period, one in the first quarter of 1968, the second in the second quarter of the same year.

By 1971 the large-scale urban riot was disappearing, and the country was becoming preoccupied with other issues—the Vietnam War, inflation, crime. But few pretended that the racial problems underlying the 1967-68 riots had disappeared. On the contrary, there was evidence or at least belief that urban black communities were becoming more disenchanted with white society. Whatever hope had been aroused by the national attention focused on the riots was seen to be frustrated, and the ordinary black adult, as distinct from the black television star or government official, was not much better off, nor apparently more satisfied, than in 1968. With King gone, the rhetoric of black spokesmen became increasingly militant, and there continued to be signs that black alienation from white society was spreading and deepening. Our third set of survey data comes from this point: mid-1971.

1

The Three Surveys

Our first set of data is drawn from interviews with 2809 black respondents, ages 16 to 69, in Detroit and fourteen other American cities. These interviews were carried out between January 6 and March 31 of 1968. We will refer to this as the *Kerner-68 Study,* since it was initiated by the President's National Advisory Commission on Civil Disorders, headed by then-Governor Otto Kerner.[1] Our initial focus will be on the 148 interviews from the Detroit subsample, but at later points the total sample, ages 21-69 will be used.

A second independent survey of black attitudes was carried out in Detroit by the Detroit Area Study (DAS) from April 24 to July 31 of 1968.[2] It included six questions from the Kerner-68 Study. This second survey, to be referred to as *DAS-68* began less than three weeks after the assassination on April 4 of Martin Luther King. The study had been planned long before the assassination, and was indeed almost called off when the assassination occurred. But certain changes (noted below) were made and interviewing began on schedule. Because the assassination occurred during the three weeks between the completion of the Kerner study and the beginning of DAS-68, a comparison of responses to the six repeated questions permits assessment of the immediate effect of the assassination on attitudes of the Detroit black adult population. The final complete sample size for DAS-68 is 619 interviews.

The third survey, also a Detroit Area Study, was carried out in 1971 from April 15 through September 26; most of the interviews were collected between May and August.[3] Unlike the previous two surveys, *DAS-71,* as we will identify it, was not primarily racial in content, but it did repeat a set of 13 questions to black respondents that had been asked in DAS-68, including the six that had also been asked in Kerner-68. Thus a compari-

---

[1]The initial results of this 15-city survey were published by the Commission in its volume *Supplemental Studies for the National Advisory Commission on Civil Disorder* (1968) and also appeared separately (Campbell and Schuman, 1968). The report includes in an appendix a brief sample description; additional information on sampling appears in Campbell (1971) and in Apprenix A of this monograph.

[2]This second survey was Detroit Area Study 965. Howard Schuman was Principal Investigator, Jean Converse and James S. House Co-Investigators. For a sampling description, see House (1968).

[3]The third survey was Detroit Area Study 46822. Otis Dudley Duncan was Principal Investigator and Howard Schuman, DAS Director. For a full sampling report, see Fischer (1972), and for an overview of results on change, see Duncan, Schuman, and Duncan (1973).

son between DAS-71 and one or both of the earlier surveys provides evidence on changes in attitudes and beliefs over approximately a three-year period. The total cross-section sample includes 405 black respondents.

Selection of the thirteen items for replication in 1971 was based on their intrinsic interest and their coverage of several important topics, as judged by the authors of the present report. The continued "meaningfulness" of items, based on some previous work with them and on a review of each in 1971, was also a factor. (We shall later note at least one failure in this review.) We gave priority to items that had been asked in both the Kerner-68 survey and the DAS-68 survey, but where this was not possible, only DAS-68 items were included because of the much greater size of that sample for baseline measurement in Detroit. All these considerations—including of course the basic constraint of prior use in 1968—provide a crude and somewhat haphazard sampling of items from a larger item universe. We will discuss below at several points what the items taken as a set seem to represent.

Equating the Three Samples

In design, all three surveys employed area probability sampling, but they differed somewhat in their definitions of the target population. Steps must be taken to render them comparable. Most obviously, the Kerner-68 study sampled fifteen cities, whereas both DAS-68 and DAS-71 sampled only the city of Detroit. This will be handled by focusing in this monograph on the Detroit data from Kerner-68. Our conclusions about attitude change are thus limited, strictly speaking, to Detroit. However, Detroit contains a large and important black population and is not atypical of most major Northern cities (see Schuman and Gruenberg, 1970, especially pp. 245-246). We shall also present at a later point data which allow comparison of Detroit with the combined fifteen cities in 1968, though we cannot demonstrate that change elsewhere has proceeded at the same pace as in Detroit. And in Chapter 6 we deal at several points substantively with the entire 15-city data set from the Kerner-68 survey.

A number of other variations in sampling and population definition also need consideration and control for these comparisons and are dealt with in detail in Appendix A. We may summarize their effects by defining our main final comparison samples as *representative of Detroit black heads and wives of heads of house, ages 21 to 69 inclusive, at each of the three points in time.*[4] The race of the interviewers also varied across the three sur-

----

[4]For sampling purposes, in families having both husband and wife, the husband was defined as "head of house." Where a single, separated, divorced, or widowed adult was head of house, he or she was defined as "head." See pages 73-74 for a discussion of other adult household members.

veys: for Kerner-68 there were black interviewers only, while race-of-interviewer was a randomized variable in each of the two DAS surveys. In certain analyses we deal only with blacks interviewed by blacks, and in other analyses both races of interviewers are included but their effects are usually controlled. At no point do we fail to take some account of race-of-interviewer.[5]

When the samples are restricted by age and household, as just described, the unweighted numbers of Detroit interviews for the three studies are as follows:

	Black inter-viewers only	Both black and white interviewers
Kerner-68	148	148 (No white interviewers)
DAS-68	439	600
DAS-71	214	342

When the full 15-city Kerner-68 sample is used, an N of 2107 is available (heads and wives, 21-69 years of age).

Changes Over Three Points in Time

All thirteen available items are presented in Table 1 with percentaged responses at the three points in time. For this basic comparison at the level of individual items, only data on blacks interviewed by blacks are shown. This is primarily to allow inclusion of the Kerner-68 data, where only black interviewers were used. In addition, there is both evidence and widespread assumption that such responses are more valid than those given to whites (Schuman and Converse, 1971), and most recent major studies of black attitudes employ black interviewers only. Later we will consider responses obtained by white interviewers as well.[6]

Eleven of the thirteen items can be considered scorable along a scale one

---

[5]Sex of respondent also requires control throughout, as do certain other features of sampling. Such controls are indicated briefly in footnotes to tables and are elaborated in Appendix A. Where weighting is necessary (primarily in DAS-68 to compensate for deliberate oversampling of high income areas), unweighted N's are always shown and are used in estimating significance, albeit with the realization that neither this no any other corrective procedure is entirely adequate.

[6]Tables of individual items paralleling the two DAS comparisons in Table 1, but for both black and white interviewer samples combined, appear in Duncan, Schuman, and Duncan (1973). Conclusions about changes in individual items are essentially the same as here.

TABLE 1 *(Sheet 1 of Table 1)*

Changes in Black Attitudes in Detroit, 1968-1971 [a]

Responses	(A) Kerner-68 (Jan., 1968) N=148	(B) DAS-68 (Apr., 1968) N=439	Difference (B-A)	(C) DAS-71 (Apr., 1971) N=214	Difference (C-B)
A. Perceptions of White Attitudes and Discrimination					
1. (80/82/178) [b] **Progress** *Some people say that over the last 10 or 15 years, there has been a lot of progress in getting rid of racial discrimination. Others say there hasn't been much real change for most (Negroes) over that time. Which do you agree with most?* [c]					
LOT OF PROGRESS	70.9	71.5		67.0	
NO CHANGE	29.1	28.5	(-0.6)	33.0	(+4.5)
N	100.0 (145)	100.0 (428)		100.0 (212)	

Footnotes are presented on Sheet 6 of this table.

TABLE 1   (*Sheet 2 of Table 1*)

Responses	(A) Kerner-68 (Jan., 1968) N=148	(B) DAS-68 (Apr., 1968) N=439	Difference (B-A)	(C) DAS-71 (Apr., 1971) N=214	Difference (C-B)
2. (127/93/182) Keep Down *On the whole, do you think most white people in Detroit want to see (Negroes) get a better break, or do they want to keep (Negroes) down, or don't they care one way or the other?*					
BETTER BREAK	41.3	42.8	(-1.7)	28.4	(+18.2)***
KEEP NEGROES DOWN	24.4	22.7		40.9	
DON'T CARE	34.4	34.5		30.7	
N	100.0 (145)	99.8 (438)		100.0 (211)	
3. (131/94/183) Trust *Do you personally feel that you can trust most white people, some white people, or none at all?*					
MOST	7.2	8.0	(+1.2)	8.2	(+6.4)*
SOME	84.0	81.8		75.4	
NONE	8.8	10.0		16.4	
N	100.0 (145)	99.8 (438)		100.0 (211)	
4. (70/80/177) Clerks *Do you think (Negro) customers who shop in the big downtown stores are treated as politely as white customers, or are they treated less politely?*					
AS POLITELY AS WHITES	76.4	67.8	(+8.6)	56.2	(+11.6)**
LESS POLITELY	23.6	32.2		43.8	
N	100.0 (135)	100.0 (417)		100.0 (208)	

TABLE 1 (*Sheet 3 of Table 1*)

Responses	(A) Kerner-68 (Jan., 1968) N=148	(B) DAS-68 (Apr., 1968) N=439	Difference (B-A)	(C) DAS-71 (Apr., 1971) N=214	Difference (C-B)
5. (—/107/185) Jobs *How many places in Detroit do you think will hire a white person before they will hire a (Negro) even though they have the same qualifications...many, some, or just a few places?*					
MANY		57.1		63.0	(-5.9)
SOME	(not asked)	27.6		19.8	
FEW		15.3		17.2	
N		100.0 (423)		100.0 (213)	
6. (—/58/176) Teachers *Do you think (Negro) teachers take more of an interest in teaching (Negro) students than white teachers do?*					
YES		43.1		38.2	(-4.9)
NO	(not asked)	56.8		61.8	
N		99.9 (394)		100.0 (202)	
B. Actions and Policies					
7. (302/152/186) Neighborhood *Would you personally prefer to live in a neighborhood with all (Negroes), mostly (Negroes), mostly whites, or a neighborhood that's mixed half and half?*					
ALL NEGRO	4.3	6.6		9.9	(+7.1)*
MOSTLY NEGRO	2.0	5.2	(+5.5)	9.0	
MOSTLY WHITE	1.2	1.3		0.8	
MIXED	57.0	56.0		62.0	
MAKES NO DIFFERENCE	35.5	31.0		18.4	
N	100.0 (147)	100.1 (437)		100.1 (213)	

TABLE 1 (Sheet 4 of Table 1)

Responses	(A) Kerner-68 (Jan., 1968) N=148	(B) DAS-68 (Apr., 1968) N=439	Difference (B-A)	(C) DAS-71 (Apr., 1971) N=214	Difference (C-B)
8. (299/239/180) Best					
USE LAWS AND PERSUASION	44.7	33.6		41.0	
USE NON-VIOLENT PROTEST	48.8	60.0		47.4	
USE VIOLENCE	6.6	6.4	(-0.2)	11.4	(+5)*
N	100.1 (140)	100.0 (430)		99.8 (210)	
9. (—/240/181) Second					
YES	(not asked)	23.5		44.4	
NO		76.6		55.7	(+20.9)***
N		100.1 (395)		100.1 (190)	
10. (—/57/175) Principals					
YES	(not asked)	43.2		43.6	
NO		56.7		56.4	(+0.4)
N		99.9 (427)		100.0 (214)	

8. (299/239/180) Best

Means *As you see it, what's the best way for (Negroes) to try to gain their rights—use laws and persuasion, use non-violent protest, or be ready to use violence?*

9. (—/240/181) Second

Means *[Asked of those not saying violence on no. 8:] If (laws and persuasion/non-violent protest) doesn't work, then do you think (Negroes) should be ready to use violence?*

10. (—/57/175) Principals

Some people say there should be (Negro) principals in schools with mostly (Negro) students because (Negroes) should have the most say in running inner city schools. Would you agree with that or not?

TABLE 1 *(Sheet 5 of Table 1)*

Responses	(A) Kerner-68 (Jan., 1968) N=148	(B) DAS-68 (Apr., 1968) N=439	Difference (B-A)	(C) DAS-71 (Apr., 1971) N=214	Difference (C-B)
11. (—/84/179) Fight for U.S. *If our country got into a big World War today, would you personally feel the United States is worth fighting for?*					
YES		85.8		90.9	
NO	(not asked)	14.2		9.1	(-5.1)
N		100.0 (423)		100.0 (208)	
C. Other Questions					
12. (—/113/184) Riot *This next question has to do with the effects of the riot in Detroit four years ago in July, 1967.*[d] *Do you think that because of that disturbance there are more whites in favor of equal rights for (Negroes), fewer whites in favor, or that the riot didn't make much difference?*					
MORE		57.8		43.4	
FEWER	(not asked)	9.0		24.4	(+15.4)***
NO DIFFERENCE		33.2		32.2	
		100.0 (434)		100.0 (206)	

TABLE 1 (*Sheet 6 of Table 1*)

Responses	(A) Kerner-68 (Jan., 1968) N=148	(B) DAS-68 (Apr., 1968) N=439	Difference (B-A)	(C) DAS-71 (Apr., 1971) N=214	Difference (C-B)
13. (—/304/391) **Entertainers**					
On another subject					
(related to how you spend					
your spare time), could ALL BLACK		42.0		44.0	(+2)
you tell me who two or MOSTLY BLACK		25.2		25.1	
three of your favorite HALF BLACK/ (not asked)					
actors or entertainers HALF WHITE		9.4		7.2	
are? [Coded for race of MOSTLY WHITE		13.5		16.2	
each entertainer ALL WHITE		9.8		7.4	
mentioned]		99.9		99.9	
		(374)		(188)	

^a All three samples are area probability cross-sections of the Detroit black population, heads of house and wives of heads of house only, ages 21-69, interviewed by black interviewers. Percentages for males and females were calculated separately and then averaged to produce the percentages shown here. Apart from sex, the only weighting occurs in DAS-68, where weights are required for "income strata," and for "interviewer" (see Appendix A). The unweighted N for each total sample is shown at the top of each column, while the unweighted N reduced by missing data is shown in parentheses for each set of percentages. Underlined responses are those in the direction of greater militancy, alienation from whites, or black consciousness. Differences between pairs of studies are shown for each such response versus all other responses to the same question; the differences are tested for significance using chi square with 1 d.f. (two categories of year and two of response), after transforming the proportions shown here into frequencies in terms of unweighted N's. Probabilities (two-tailed) are: *p<.05; **p<.01; ***p<.001

^b Codebook variable numbers for each study are shown for reference purposes. Item numbers 1 to 13 will be used in this report, as will the verbal tag shown in bold face for each item.

^c The racial term employed was adapted to respondent preference. See footnote 9 of this chapter.

^d This first sentence was omitted in DAS-68, since the question followed several others on "last July's disturbance."

end of which represents heightened "black consciousness," "militancy," "alienation from whites," and related attitudes. Responses so considered are underlined in Table 1, and the percentage differences over time are shown. These eleven items are organized on an a priori basis in two panels: one (A) comprising "perceptions" of the way America appears to the respondent, the other (B) comprising "policies" or "actions" to which the respondent subscribes. A third panel (C) includes two miscellaneous items, one of which (effects of the 1968 Detroit riot) is difficult to classify in terms of expected direction of change, while the other (entertainers) is completely non-ideological in overt content and will be treated separately.

Was There Attitude Change Due to the Assassination?

Six questions were asked in both the Kerner-68 survey and the DAS-68 survey—the first ending just a few days before the assassination of Martin Luther King, the second beginning just a few days after the assassination. Four of these questions (1, 2, 3, 8) show essentially *no* change, while two questions (4 and 7) show some change in the expected direction, though not enough to register statistical significance.[7] However, the four items which do *not* shift are exactly the ones most relevant to the assassination. Two deal directly with perceptions of white hostility, notably item 2 on whether most whites want to keep (Negroes) down. One item concerns the sense of overall progress in civil rights—which certainly received a setback with the assassination of the foremost civil rights leader of modern times. Finally, one item turns on the need for blacks to rely on violence to gain their rights. The fact that not one of these four items shows even slight effects of the assassination strongly suggests that such attitude change did not occur.

The two items that do give some evidence of change deal with attitudes further removed from events like the assassination. Why should perceptions of discrimination by store clerks (item 4), the one difference approaching statistical significance ($X^2 = 3.4$, 1 d.f., $p < .10$) be affected by King's murder? A shift toward exclusive black association (item 7) is more

---

[7]Conventional tests of significance are employed throughout, even though all three samples made some use of clustering by block. Design effects are quite slight in these single city samples for most of the variables considered here (of an order of 1.1 or 1.2, as reported by Fields, 1970-71), but this means that such tests are a bit less conservative than they appear and that borderline levels of significance should be treated with caution. The same caution is required by use of multiple tests in a survey analysis of this sort, but we do think it valuable to report such tests of significance. Care has been taken to make use of replication and other evidence to clarify borderline levels of significance ($.10 > p > .01$).

plausibly connected with the assassination, but in the absence of significance and of effects on other equally plausible items, this is a doubtful conclusion. Taken as a whole, the results seem better interpreted as failing to reveal systematic effects on black attitudes as a result of the assassination. The DAS-68 data may be picking up more general movement on the two items that show non-significant trends, since both exhibit further and more clearly reliable change between 1968 and 1971, but there is little reason to associate the earlier 1968 differences as such with the assassination. (See also Meyer, 1969.)

All this is not to assert that the assassination failed to move blacks deeply, but only that it did not *immediately* shift basic attitudes toward greater militancy or alienation from whites. Indeed, we have other evidence that the immediate effect of the assassination was *conservative,* as shown by the results for the following two questions that were asked in DAS-68 just after the assassination:[8]

Since Dr. King's assassination, do you think there are more whites in favor of equal rights, fewer whites, or isn't there much change?

Some people are saying that the assassination of Martin Luther King will drive (Negroes) and whites further apart. Others think that it will bring them closer together. Which do you think will probably happen?

1. More whites 59%	1. Further apart 9%
2. Fewer 4	2. Closer together 68
3. Not much change 35	3. No change (volunteered). .20
Don't know 2	Don't know 3
100%	100%

Despite the well-known hazards of interpreting absolute item marginals, the implication of these two distributions deserves note. The immediate reaction of the black population as a whole to the assassination was not sudden disillusionment with whites, but rather a belief that this tragic event would spur positive feelings and actions between blacks and whites. It is no wonder then that our change questions, which were repeated at the same point, do not reflect a shift toward militancy as an immediate result of King's death. Over a longer period the assassination may well have had an alienating effect, but that is another question and one we cannot hope to answer in specific causal terms with these data.

----

[8]These results are based on 439 cases from the original DAS-68 sample of 619. Excluded are respondents interviewed by whites and all those over 69 years of age.

Was There Attitude Change Between 1968 and 1971?

We shall at this point assume that the two earlier studies do not point to short-term general attitude change in early 1968 among blacks. What of the three years between 1968 and 1971? For this purpose we will use mainly the DAS-68 sample for baseline data, since from that study all 13 replicated questions are available for comparison. (The DAS-68 sample is also much larger than the Kerner-68 Detroit sample, and addition of the latter data would not greatly strengthen the 1968-1971 comparison.) The evidence for attitude change over this three-year period (Columns B and C in Table 1) is persuasive, although not without some puzzling features.

Nine of the eleven directional questions presented in panels A and B of Table 1 show shifts in the direction of greater alienation from white society, greater black consciousness, greater militancy. Six of these shifts are significant beyond the .05 level, with two showing chi square values (23.1 for item 2 and 26.0 for item 9) far beyond the probability of chance occurrence. Thus it seems safe to conclude that black attitudes changed in *some* important ways over the three-year period. Moreover, the average (mean and median) change of +6 percent for these eleven items taken as a whole is not slight in absolute terms for such a short period. Over ten years, for example, it would lead to a 20 percent shift in black attitudes on this set of items—no small change for America if attitudes count for anything.

At the level of individual items, one of the largest differences involves an unusually incisive question (item 2) on the fundamental nature of black-white relations, as shown in Figure 1. In 1968 some 43 percent of Detroit blacks believed that most whites "want to see (Negroes) get a better break," but this had dropped to 28 percent in 1971, while the percentage believing that most whites "want to keep (Negroes) down" rose from 23 percent to 41 percent over the same period.[9] The 1968 Report of the National Advisory Commission on Civil Disorders concluded that: "Our Nation is moving toward two societies, one black, one white—separate and unequal." (p.1) Whatever the validity of that statement as a projection of long-term attitude change for whites,[10] it fits the change in *perception by blacks* of the nature of white attitudes and intentions. That in itself is a sign of

---

[9]Although we print "Negro" as the term used in these questions, all three surveys contained instructions to interviewers to use the racial term (e.g., "black," "Negro," "colored") preferred by each respondent insofar as he or she indicated a preference. Parentheses are used in printing questions to indicate this variability.

[10]It does *not* fit what we know about the trends in white attitudes; see Campbell (1971) and Greeley and Sheatsley (1971). Whether it fits change in other areas such as economic status is not entirely clear; see Farley and Hermalin (1972).

increased separation, for "if men define situations as real, they are real in their consequences" (Thomas and Thomas, 1928). This not blindly to assume that the change in black perceptions is an unhealthy one; it may indicate movement toward a more realistic view of whites, a view which could also facilitate black mobilization and organization for political and economic pressure in other areas of life.

FIGURE 1

Changes in "Keep Down" Item, 1968-1971

"On the whole do you think most white people in Detroit want to see (Negroes) get a better break, or do they want to keep (Negroes) down, or don't they care one way or the other?" (DAS-68 and DAS-71)

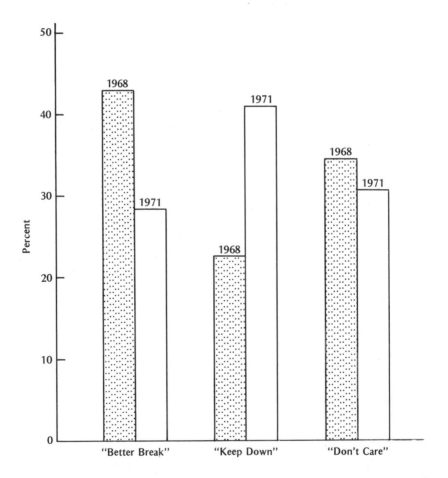

That there is increasing skepticism of white behavior is suggested by another highly significant difference between 1968 and 1971. White sales-clerks (item 4) are accused of discriminatory treatment by 12 percent more respondents in 1971 than in mid-1968 (and by 20 percent more than in the Kerner-68 survey). It seems unlikely that this form of white discrimination has actually increased over the 1968-1971 period, although it is possible that a greater proportion of blacks are shopping in general downtown stores and thus being exposed to discourteous treatment. Quite likely the change reflects increased scrutiny of white actions by blacks, as well as possibly increased black presumption that discrimination does exist every-where. General presumption of discrimination is apparently not the only factor, however, since the change from 1968 to 1971 is slighter and non-significant on a similar item dealing with employment discrimination (item 5). We are unwise to depend too heavily on the reliability of such item differences, but the specific result on store clerks seems to fit best a model that stresses an increasing "sensitivity" of blacks to nuances in white actions which reveal or suggest prejudice.

Turning now to the more conative items in Table 1, there is only a rela-tively small difference of borderline significance ($x^2 = 4.6$, 1 d.f.) on item 8 dealing with readiness to use violence to secure black rights.[11] However, a more latent question on this same possibility (item 9) shows a much more marked change. In 1968 only 23 percent of the black population was willing to consider violence if other means fail, but in 1971 the figure rose to 44 percent. Taken at face value, the pattern on the two items suggests that relatively few blacks (some 11 percent) were ready at this point to advocate violence, but that a much larger proportion have moved to a position where violence is no longer rejected as an ultimately necessary strategy.

The items which show little or even negative change over the three-year period are also of interest. Blacks are *not* more likely in the later year to claim that white teachers are disinterested in black students (item 6). Nor is there any visible increase in willingness to make race the criterion for selection of school principals (item 10). Black consciousness does seem to appear in another question, that on neighborhood housing preference

---

[11]This item includes two non-violent alternatives which were apparently not distinguished in terms of militancy by respondents. Although "non-violent pro-test" was intended to be seen as more militant than use of "laws and persuasion," in fact the term "non-violent" probably attracted respondents who wished to reject violence, with the word "protest" ignored. Bearing this out, there is no relation between responses on these two alternatives taken alone and responses on item 9, nor between the first two responses and responses on other militancy items. For all our analysis of question 8, therefore, we collapse the first two alternatives and contrast them to the third as an indication of unwillingness or willingness to con-sider violence as a means "to gain . . . rights."

(item 7), where there is a significant increase ($x^2 = 5.6, 1$ d.f., $p < .05$) in the desire to live in mainly or wholly black neighborhoods.[12] These item differences suggest a distinction between "black consciousness" as expressed in personal preferences for association with blacks, and "black power" as expressed in willingness to discriminate publicly against whites, as in the school principal item.[13]

Three other items deserve special note. First, an open question (no. 13) on "favorite actors or entertainers" was coded in terms of the race of each such entertainer mentioned. If implicit preference for black entertainers represents a manifestation of cultural "black consciousness," then there is no evidence in Table 1 of an increase in this cultural emphasis between 1968 and 1971. Even more surprising is the lack of significant change in willingness to fight for the United States in a major war. Over a period of growing disillusionment with the Vietnam War, one might well have expected increased black resistance to military service even in the hypothetical context of a major war. But item 11 of Table 1 shows that actually the insignificant change that did occur was in the opposite direction—toward *more* willingness by blacks to fight for the U.S. The results for this item are perhaps the most puzzling of all those in Table 1, especially since we will later see (Table 2) that "No" to this question is indeed associated with other items indicating militancy or alienation from white

---

[12]Item 7 on residential preference is unusually complex, with four proffered alternatives plus a fifth given spontaneously by a surprisingly large number of people. Separate analysis of this item against a number of other racial items indicates that the "all Negro" and "mostly Negro" alternatives tend to be similar in direction of associations with other items, although the first alternative almost always appears higher in "black consciousness." Thus grouping these two alternatives as shown in Table 1 makes sense. It is even clearer from such analysis that "mixed" and makes no difference" are essentially indistinguishable in relation to other questions, although it is puzzling that one of these latter responses rises slightly in popularity over time, while the other is falling sharply. But failing construct validation of their distinctiveness, we treat them as part of the same basic orientation and consider only the net decline over both of them, along with that to the "mostly white" alternative.

[13]One might wish to qualify this distinction by noting the fact that already in 1968 a much larger percentage seemed willing to support the automatic placement of black principals in black schools than chose racial separation in terms of neighborhood in either 1968 *or* 1971. Such comparisons between questions are extremely hazardous, however, because the marginal distributions are so highly affected by various aspects of question wording (see Chapter 2 below.) But we would do well to keep in mind absolute levels of response, as well as changes in these levels.

society. But there is little reason to doubt the validity of the lack of change shown for this item.[14]

For all the items we have discussed thus far, a clear prediction of direction of change could be made in advance. Item 12, however, was one we could only guess at before seeing results, although it turns out to show one of the largest attitude shifts of all. In 1968 the majority of Detroit blacks felt the 1967 riot had spurred white sympathies. This may well have been due to the same assumption that underlay response to the questions on King's assassination discussed earlier—that *any* event which dramatized injustice against blacks would stimulate white understanding and support. In 1971, however, a significantly larger proportion of blacks than in 1968 believed the riot had actually lessened white support. Perhaps this disillusionment over time had had something to do with the sharp decrease in the occurrence and even talk of riots in Detroit and elsewhere since the end of the sixties. If the urban riot is conceived of as a form of protest, blacks increasingly look back on it as unsuccessful in terms of its effects on white attitudes.

We have concentrated here on items that show large and significant difference between 1968 and 1971, or on the other hand on items that show no difference at all. Items showing smaller and non-significant differences, such as question 1, are more difficult to interpret. It is tempting to regard such differences (4.5 percent in the case of item 1) as real but simply too slight to register as significant with these relatively small samples. But the two "negative" differences in Table 1 (for items 6 and 11) are of comparable magnitude, yet probably should be regarded as departing from zero only because of sampling error. It seems wisest to refrain from interpreting single-item marginal differences in Table 1 where they are non-significant. (We will, however, use all eleven directional items in an index for further analysis, as well as study the items separately at later points.)

We can summarize the main results for 1968 and 1971 as showing difference, and therefore presumably change, in two major ways: (1) over the 1968-1971 period, a substantially larger proportion of the Detroit black population came to perceive whites as antagonistic; (2) blacks, perhaps because of this increased perception of antagonism, began to entertain for

---

[14]While the Fight for U.S. item can no doubt be criticized as to wording, there is indirect evidence to support the finding of no change. On another DAS-71 question concerning a possible future "Communist revolution" in South America, there is no significant overall difference between blacks and whites as far as willingness to support American intervention. This fits the finding reported elsewhere that black opposition to the Vietnam War, while greater than white opposition, was apparently not distinctively ideological in content (Schuman, 1972c).

the first time in interviews the possibility of violence as an eventual outcome of racial conflict in America. This is not to say that violent conflict was more imminent in 1971—or at this writing—than it was in 1968. We are dealing with beliefs and attitudes, not with behavior or even behavioral intention. Division seems clearly sharper in 1971 than in 1968, but where that will lead is not revealed by these data.

2

SOME METHODOLOGICAL PROBLEMS IN EVALUATING ITEM CHANGE

Before proceeding to a more detailed analysis of the change items, several important methodological problems bearing on Table 1 deserve brief discussion.

Ceiling, Bandwagon, and Other Effects

It is possible that changes occur more easily from some initial response levels than from others. Several psychological and statistical models can be adduced, symbolized by terms such as "ceiling effects," "bandwagon effects," and other presumed mechanisms. Without attempting a formal treatment of Table 1 in these terms, we may note whether there is substantial empirical evidence for any such mechanism in these data. Below are the twelve directional items from Table 1, ordered by the percentage level of their DAS-68 *underlined* response, and showing also the increment (or decrement) to 1971:

Item	Percentage in DAS-68	Percentage change to 1971
8	6.4	5.0
3	10.0	6.4
7	11.8	7.1
11	14.2	-5.1
2	22.7	18.2
9	23.5	20.9
1	28.5	4.5
4	32.2	11.6
13	42.0	2.0
6	43.1	-4.9
10	43.2	0.4
5	57.1	5.9

We can note first that the initial percentage level of response ranges from close to zero to just above 50 percent. This is largely a consequence of two item-construction considerations invoked in 1968. One involved the attempt to measure certain attitudes which were deemed important but not unexpectedly were rare (for example, positive orientation toward violence). Except for that goal, there was a general strategy to avoid so far as possible highly skewed items. Together the two considerations led to absence of items on which there might already have been extremely high response in the direction in which change was presumed to be proceeding. Thus, a ceiling effect is unlikely, since none of the items approach 100 percent in either year *in the direction of expected change.*

The actual listing shown here suggests a slight negative relationship (r = -.19, n.s.), and somewhat more clearly a tendency for change to be greatest in the 20 percent to 30 percent range. Where the black population was already divided roughly in half in 1968, there is little or no change in 1971, so that we do not at all have a picture of movement toward a monolithic black public opinion. Rather, the changes between 1968 and 1971 tend, in terms of the question wordings used, to divide the black population closer to the fifty-fifty mark on a series of important issues. These speculations must be taken with some grains of salt,[1] but they do suggest that the change going on among blacks leads to variation in attitude *within* the black community, as well as between blacks and whites. They also indicate

---

[1]There is the problem of possible regression effects for items that were "extreme" in 1968, and also the problem of lack of exact comparability of a given percentage difference from one base level to another. Larger problems of question wording are dealt with in the next secion.

the importance of attempting to locate the sources of this variation within the black population.

Question Wording

Our discussion has touched several times upon marginal percentages for individual items. For example, we saw earlier that preference for mainly black neighborhoods has risen significantly between 1968 and 1971, while preference for black principals in all-black schools did not change over the same period; but we also saw that the latter preference was already in 1968—and remained in 1971—much higher than the former. One might almost speculate that the black preference level on the one item was simply "catching up" with the other.

Yet the hazards of taking marginal percentages as meaningful in themselves was also noted. A good example of this danger is available for the item on school principals shown in Table 1 (item 10). A differently worded question on the same basic issue was asked in the Kerner-68 survey and produced the following distribution for Detroit:

> *"Suppose there is a public school that is attended mostly*
> *by (Negro) children—do you think the principal should be*
> *a (Negro), a white person, or that his race should not make*
> *any difference?"*
> 1. Should be a Negro...................... 12%
> 2. No difference.......................... 87
> 3. Should be a white..................... 1
> ────
> 100%
> N (146)

While the two school principal items are quite different in wording, they both ask whether black schools should, ipso facto, have black principals. The earlier tabled item indicates that 44 percent of the black population favored such a position, yet the question shown here indicates the figure to be only 12 percent. The *difference of 32 percent* is larger than *any* of the changes over time presented in Table 1, and demonstrates vividly the influence of question wording on response levels.[2] Moreover, the Kerner-68 school principal item shown here is worded more closely in

───────────

[2]We cannot completely reject the possibility that there is some real shift on this issue between the two 1968 surveys, but it is highly unlikely that change over a few months could approach 32 percent when there is no change at all over the 1968-1971 period for the tabled item.

form to the forced-choice neighborhood preference item (number 7), and thus if there is to be any between-item comparison in marginals, it should probably be for these two items. Obviously any comparison at all of absolute item marginals is risky, given this variability due to wording.

Survey analysts generally seek to avoid such wording problems by claiming not to deal with absolute item marginals, though this claim is not always lived up to in practice.[3] But even comparisons of the same item over time cannot free us entirely from a concern with question wording. We have already seen that of two items (8 and 9) on violence in Table 1, one shows relatively slight change of borderline significance, the other a large and highly significant change. If asked whether or not acceptance of violence by blacks has increased over time, a balanced answer must draw on both items—and indeed, in theory, on other conceivable items on the same subject. Likewise we cannot be certain that the school principal item from the Kerner-68 survey would have shown the same lack of change as did the one from DAS-68 that we actually replicated. Consideration of item wording in change studies cannot be avoided entirely.

Finally, one cannot even assume that associations between items and background factors such as education will always be stable when marginals are not. For one thing, when marginals shift drastically, levels of association are likely to be altered also. But the point goes deeper, for even the *nature* of relationships can sometimes depend upon item wording. Thus we will see later that the DAS-68 school principal item shows a significant association with education (the less educated are more in favor of a black principal), yet the Kerner-68 principal item reveals no sign of such a relationship; indeed, as is developed elsewhere (Schuman and Duncan, 1974), the resulting interaction among education, wording of item, and response to item seems to be statistically reliable. The explanation for this difference in relational direction is probably that the DAS-68 principal item is "loaded" toward easy acceptance, because of its agreeing format and the persuasive "argument" it contains as part of the question, as against the less loaded wording of the Kerner-68 version. This difference primarily affects the overall marginal distribution of the former item, but it apparently has a noticeably stronger effect on the least educated segments of the population.

We strongly suspect that the DAS-68 principal question is more problematic than others in Table 1, and thus produces almost the maximum format and wording effect one can obtain in surveys. But the more general

---

[3]For a recent survey report that offers interpretations of absolute marginals, see Blumenthal, *et al.* (1972). For a direct attempt to make positive use of item marginals, see Schuman (1972a).

point nevertheless holds: the need to avoid too much stress on results based only on a single item. The usual way out of this difficulty is to work with an index made up of numerous items on the same subject. Exactly this approach will be taken below in part, although we cannot claim to deal in a simple sense with any single "subject" or dimension. But a little thought will show that even this strategy, while in many ways an improvement (and in some ways a loss), cannot prevent wording and format effects that are systematic over all or most items. In sum, judgment, replication *across* items, and constructive skepticism remain essential. We have tried to maintain a balance between such considerations and straightforward substantive conclusions in the pages that follow.

Question Context

Analysis of attitude change over time points up another classic issue of survey methodology—that of the influence of question order and context on responses. Even where the very same item is repeated in two surveys, it is almost always *preceded* by different sets of questions. This was certainly true of the surveys under consideration here, for both the Kerner and the DAS-68 questionnaires were almost entirely concerned with racial issues, while the small set of racial questions in DAS-71 followed long sections on ostensibly nonracial matters. Even *within* the set of DAS-71 items, previous orderings could not be preserved because of omission in 1971 of some earlier questions.

Not much is known about context effects in surveys, and in any case they may well be specific to particular types of items or particular contexts. In the DAS-71 survey, we included a number of experimental variations in question placement, made possible by printing two forms of the questionnaire. The forms were administered randomly, with approximately half the total sample receiving Form A and half Form B. One strategic racial item, the entertainer question (item 13 in Table 1), was involved in such systematic variation in ordering.[4]

The entertainer item was chosen for this experiment because it had already been shown to be quite sensitive to another kind of contextual cue, namely, race of interviewer (Schuman and Converse, 1971). In addition, it is an "indirect" question: entertainer's race is not mentioned explicitly to respondents as a goal of the question, but is simply coded after responses

---

[4]Only this single race-related context experiment is dealt with here. A more general report on context effects over a number of questions in DAS-71 is planned. For an earlier study of context effects, see Bradburn and Mason (1964).

are obtained. It seemed quite possible that alerting or not alerting respondents to the purpose of the question would influence response patterns. Following this assumption, in Form B of the 1971 survey the entertainer item was located at the end of the whole series of racial questions, while in Form A it preceded all other questions on race. The hypothesis was that black respondents would mention a larger proportion of black entertainers to Form B than to Form A, since the Form B context both stimulates race-related attitudes and alerts respondents to the relevance of race to the entertainer question.

The DAS-71 results for race of entertainer by form are shown below, with race-of-interviewer controlled:

"Could you tell me who two or three of your favorite actors or entertainers are?" (DAS-71)

	Form A		Form B	
	Black inter-viewers	White inter-viewers	Black inter-viewers	White inter-viewers
Race of Entertainer				
Mention blacks only	41.1%	12.3%	33.3%	15.9%
Mainly black	20.5	18.5	25.5	20.6
Black and white equally	8.0	9.2	5.9	6.4
Mainly white	13.4	24.6	15.7	20.6
Whites only	7.1	18.5	4.9	19.0
Don't know	9.8	16.9	14.7	17.5
	99.9%	100%	100%	100%
N	(112)	(65)	(102)	(63)

The DAS survey confirms the *interviewer effect* discovered in 1968: within each form, black interviewers elicit black entertainers significantly more often than do whites. Although the race-of-interviewer relationship may appear stronger in Form A ($x^2 = 19.1$, 4 d.f., p $<$ .001) than in Form B ($x^2 = 13.0$, 4 d.f., p $<$ .02),[5] the hypothesis of three-way interaction among form, interviewer's race, and entertainer's race is not confirmed ($x^2 = 1.6$, 4 d.f., n.s.).[6] Finally, form—that is, the location of item—is not re-

[5]"Don't know" responses were excluded from these calculations. The statistics here are likelihood-ratio chi squares.

[6]If the entertainer item is collapsed to all-black vs. others, then $x^2 = 0.9$, 1 d.f., is still non-significant.

lated directly to entertainer's race ($X^2 = 1.7$, 4 d.f., n.s.).

Thus, we conclude that context does not affect the entertainer item, either in terms of marginal percentages or relation to race-of-interviewer. Since the entertainer item was chosen for this experimental manipulation precisely because of its probable vulnerability to context, it seems likely that the other racial items in our study are also relatively free of such effects. Context effects, unlike question wording effects, do not appear to be a major problem for our analysis. The issue of race-of-interviewer touched on above does require further discussion, but we defer this until a later point.

Interpretations of Items by Respondents: Random Probes

In addition to formal considerations of item format, wording, and context, there is the more complex problem of determining whether respondents understand individual survey questions and interpret them within the same frame of reference as the investigators. Indeed, questions can seem equally meaningful to both parties in an interview without that meaning necessarily being shared.

For the Kerner-68 survey a methodological procedure outlined elsewhere (Schuman, 1966) was included to obtain additional information on how respondents interpret the questions. In essence, the technique consists of identifying a random subsample of about fifty respondents for each closed question and asking this subsample to explain in their own words why they gave the closed response they did. These explanations come after the closed question in reply to a non-directive probe such as: "Could you explain a little what you mean when you say that?" Recorded verbatim by interviewers, the set of representative probe responses to each item provides insight into how respondents interpret questions and what they had in mind in choosing a particular alternative. Since the probes yield "after the fact" explanations, they cannot be taken as literal validation, but they do offer a kind of insight into question meaning that is frequently lacking in analysis based entirely on closed survey items. They provide some of the advantages of open questions—without some of their disadvantages—to the large-scale structured survey.

Thus for each of the six questions in Table 1 that were included in the Kerner-68 survey, we have some fifty "random probe" interpretations of response choice by respondents. (The fifty respondents differ for each question.) Appendix B presents a representative set of these interpretations for each item, and we here briefly summarize the findings and give selected examples. Item numbers and labels refer to Table 1, where complete question wording is presented.

1. **"Progress."** Those who choose "lot of progress" show good understanding of the question. About two-thirds of the explanations focus on concrete issues of jobs, housing, and education—for example: "There are a lot of places where Negroes now can work." Those who choose "not much change" also speak in terms of concrete issues, such as "We can do the same job as whites but get unequal pay." Hardly any mention is made by respondents of largely symbolic changes such as Supreme Court decisions, which figure more heavily in scholarly accounts of civil rights progress. Thus respondent frame of reference is slightly different for this question than some readers may assume, though this does not present problems for our own subsequent use of the item.

2. **"Keep Down."** The "better break" response is well understood and includes not only specific issues ("They are giving us a little better job . . . are changing things around.") but also more general support ("I have white friends who have given me compliments, encouragement, and awards for my efforts in sports."). Not all the explanations for the "better break" choice are so unqualified: "Some are not too prejudiced against Negroes." The alternative at the other extreme, "keep down," yields clear-cut responses such as "Hate, that's why they want to keep the Negro down. Whites, some of them really hate." and "They don't like Negroes in good positions . . . it threatens their security." The "don't care" alternative produces a number of responses similar to the "keep down" alternative ("A white person does not want a Negro to get a high position."), plus some that fit more specifically the category label ("On the whole most people don't think about the problem.").In retrospect, in collapsing the three alternatives to two, we might better have combined "don't care" with keep down, rather than with "better break" as is done throughout most of this volume.

3. **"Trust."** 'Trust most white people" yields clear explanations: "Oh, you can trust most people. I don't see that race has anything to do with it." Most of the "trust some" and "trust none" responses are equally straightforward ("Some are really friendly and nice, others are not [and] dislike you on general principle." "They only want to use the black man."). But several responses are non-racial in implication ("Because I don't

trust nobody at all—not nobody no matter what race."), and it is clear that this question taps a general misanthropy factor, as well as racial distrust.

4. **"Clerks."** Respondents who see equal politeness in stores sometimes qualify it ("They want my money, so treat all people alike"), but otherwise the response is unambiguous. Those who say "less politely" give varied but clear responses: "They pass by me to wait on another white," "Often you are looked at as though you are trying to steal something," "They treat Negroes so cold."

7. **"Neighborhood Preference."** This question was followed by a general probe (*Why do you feel that way?*) to the entire sample, rather than to only a random subset. The complete codes and percentage distributions are included in Appendix B. Those preferring black neighborhoods most often speak in terms of comfort ("get along better with your own") but sometimes mention fear of white hostility ("would be afraid of being stoned in a white neighborhood"). Those who prefer mixed neighborhoods explain their response most frequently in terms of "coming to understand one another," but some also emphasize the purely physical and service characteristics of neighborhoods ("they'd have to give you the same services they give the whites") and others simply assert that race is an irrelevant factor in choosing a neighborhood. Thus explanations to this question are quite varied, suggesting that it taps several factors, though none of these can be considered to represent misunderstanding. Rather we are dealing here within a single question with a more complex issue than for most other questions. This may account for its somewhat lower correlation (see Chapter 3, Table 2) with other index items.[7]

---

[7]Unfortunately this follow-up open question could not be repeated in 1971. It is possible in a case like this that even where the closed pattern of responses remains largely unchanged, the reasons, or at least explanations, for such responses may shift. Thus, those choosing mixed neighborhoods may increasingly explain their choice in terms of improved services rather than racial harmony. The point seems well worth testing in change studies, although the problems of obtaining comparability in coding should not be underestimated. (See Duncan, Schuman, and Duncan, 1973, pp. 36-39).

8. **"Best Means."** The violence alternative to this question is quite clear and uniform in meaning: "They've been singing and praying all their lives. It will have to be violence, I do believe." The other two alternatives, however, are explained in ways that vary from positive assertion that there is a "better means" than violence ("If Negroes unite, they can bring enough pressure so that they can get their rights through the courts.") to what are simply negative reactions to the mention violence ("Violence won't do anything but get you killed.") to some probable misunderstandings ("Most people will obey laws and do as they are told."). The basic differentiation between accepting and rejecting the possibility of violence is generally clear in these responses, but the attempt in the original question to distinguish "laws and persuasion" from "non-violent protest" is not very successful. The latter failure in distinction is confirmed by analysis (Chapter 1, footnote 11), and therefore we have merged these two alternatives in opposition to the alternative "be ready to use violence" in subsequent use of this item.

Overall, these six questions were well understood by most respondents, though sometimes in ways not fully anticipated by the investigators. We feel confident that most people answered most of the questions within the broadly intended frame of reference. This was by no means inevitable, and at a later point (Chapter 6) we will see a striking example of a failure in communication between question writer and respondent which leads to analytic perplexities that are not resolved until the root cause in misunderstanding is appreciated.

3

ITEM INTERCORRELATIONS AND
THE CONSTRUCTION OF AN INDEX

Item Intercorrelations

We have spoken several times of a single "direction" to the main items in Table 1. If indeed the items are to some degree measures of the same construct, whatever its label, they should all be positively intercorrelated. Moreover, if one assumes that a more encompassing ideology of black consciousness is developing rapidly in America, the items should be more highly intercorrelated in 1971 than in 1968. Or subsets of the items might be more clearly delineated at one point in time than another. As a practical matter, it would be easier to proceed in analysis with a larger and more reliable index than with a set of separate items; but this presupposes item intercorrelations high enough to justify construction of such an index. The intercorrelations in Table 2 provide evidence on both the substantive and the methodological issues.

The table gives results separately for the two years (DAS-68 below the diagonal, DAS-71 above), using all Detroit respondents (heads and wives only), whether interviewed by blacks or whites. Only the eleven items that were thought to have a clear ideological direction are shown here; that is, those in panels A and B of Table 1. In addition, an index constructed by summing the 11 items is included in each matrix and will be discussed below. [1]

---

[1] For the purposes of both correlation and index construction, each item was converted to a three-point scale. Three points were assigned to the response(s) higher in militancy, black consciousness, or alienation; one point to the response(s) lower on such dimensions; and two points to "don't know" and similar missing data. These three-point scales were intercorrelated using product-moment coefficients to produce the figures in Table 2. (Variables 8 and 9 required special treatment, since 9 was contingent on 8; for these correlations, persons choosing "violence" on 8 were coded also as choosing violence on 9, even though they had not actually been asked the latter item.) To test the effect of the inclusion of missing data on the correlations, five of the eleven variables were also intercorrelated without missing data. For both years the new correlations varied from the old by no more than .03 of a point.

TABLE 2

Intercorrelations Among Eleven Items in 1968 and 1971*

	1	2	3	4	5	6	7	8	9	10	11	Index
1. Progress	—	.18	.11	.24	.16	.14	.02	.18	.20	.10	.28	.51
2. Keep down	.18	—	.20	.22	.14	.17	.16	.21	.27	.11	.08	.53
3. Trust	.12	.19	—	.10	.14	.09	.22	.25	.17	.14	.06	.42
4. Clerks	.14	.14	.09	—	.12	.07	.12	.12	.11	.07	.16	.46
5. Jobs	.17	.14	.14	.12	—	.10	.18	.08	.16	.11	.09	.45
6. Teachers	.08	.08	.09	.12	.23	—	.12	.08	.19	.32	.09	.48
7. Neighborhood	.07	.04	.07	.08	.06	.10	—	.11	.18	.23	.12	.44
8. Best means	.24	.10	.10	.12	.15	.18	.07	—	.37	.17	.17	.47
9. Second means	.20	.13	.16	.04	.15	.11	.04	.41	—	.26	.16	.60
10. Principals	.06	.02	.03	.08	.09	.38	.20	.11	.14	—	.12	.52
11. Fight for U.S.	.28	.10	.17	.23	.13	.14	.03	.27	.28	.10	—	.38
Index	.51	.42	.37	.44	.51	.53	.30	.48	.52	.48	.51	—

1968 (below the diagonal)   1971 (above the diagonal)

*Correlations for DAS-71 are shown above the diagonal; correlations for DAS-68 are shown below the diagonal. The unweighted N for DAS-68 is 600; the N for DAS-71 is 342. The numbering here follows that in Table 1, where the complete wording for each item is shown.

All the inter-item correlations in Table 2 are positive for both years, with a mean of .136 for DAS-68 and of .155 for DAS-71.[2] Thus a slight increase in cohesiveness of the items appears in the later year, but it is non-significant and trivial in size.[3] Our clearest conclusion is that the eleven items are all intercorrelated at a low positive level in both years, with no reliable change in average association over time.[4]

The distinction between "perception" and "action" items that was used in organizing Table 1 turns out to be a distinction that does not make much of a difference. The mean correlations within and between these two sets are:

	1968	1971
Among six Perception items	.14	.15
Among five Action items	.16	.19
Between Perception and Action items	.13	.15

---

[2]If only respondents interviewed by black interviewers are used, with appropriate weighting for DAS-68 to represent the total Detroit black population, the mean correlations are. 129 and .144 for DAS-68 and DAS-71, respectively.

[3]There is considerable risk of capitalizing on random error if we focus on changes over time in *each* bivariate correlation. Nevertheless, it is worth noting the larger changes appearing in Table 2, as reflected by the item-scale coefficients for the two years. It is interesting that the largest increase (+.14) in item-scale correlation between 1968 and 1971 occurs for item 7 on preferred racial composition of neighborhoods. If we conceive of this item as reflecting positive "black consciousness," as distinct from items dealing with feelings of alienation and militancy, then it is probably true that black consciousness is a more recently developed emphasis, and it is plausible that the item did become more closely linked to the other index questions between 1968 and 1971. On the other hand, the sharpest decrease in correlation over the three-year period involves item 11 on Fight for the U.S. (-.13), and for this change we have no plausible interpretation and are inclined to attribute it to chance variation.

[4]We also calculated for DAS-68 the mean intercorrelation for the eleven items at each of three age levels and at each of three educational levels. Converse (1964) suggests that attitudinal integration is greater among those more "involved" in a political subject area, and it seemed possible that this would be the case for younger and better educated respondents. For the three age levels (ages 21-35, 36-49, 50+), the differences in mean correlation are small, non-monotonic, and not in the predicted direction. For the three educational groups (0-11, 12, 13+ years of education), the college educated do show a higher mean intercorrelation (.19) than either of the other two categories (.13 and .12), although the difference is not significant (p > .20). Given the predicted trend, we repeated the calculations for the six items in the Kerner-68 total 15-city sample, where the N is 2106. The mean correlations for the same three educational groups are .14, .10, and .14, respectively, and none of the paired differences approach significance (p > .10). Thus the hypothesis is not confirmed for either set of items.

Thus items are about as highly correlated across the hypothesized subsets as they are within them.

Nor do other sharply distinctive subsets emerge from study of the intercorrelations in Table 2. Simple cluster analyses were performed on both the 1968 and 1971 matrices, but produced no clear-cut clusters of items beyond pairs. The two items dealing with violence (8 and 9) form a relatively separate cluster in each year, though this is partly due to the contingent relation of one to the other. Two other item pairs (1 and 11, 6 and 10) also are somewhat distinct in both years, but they lack sufficient conceptual value to warrant separate treatment. Moreover, even these three pairs are related almost as well to the other items, and it seems justifiable to treat them tentatively as part of the larger set of eleven for the purpose of an overall view of attitude change and its correlates.

Following this judgment, the eleven items, each scored one to three, were summed in order to create a single index. The initial range of the index was 11 to 33, but this was collapsed by combining adjacent scores to yield final scores varying from 1 to 11.[5] Table 2 shows that all eleven items are correlated at least moderately with the total index, the range being .30 to .53 in 1968 and .38 to .60 in 1971. No item is consistently low for both years, nor is there any item that is both relatively low in item-scale correlation and conceptually distant from the total set. Reliabilities (internal consistency) estimated from mean inter-item correlations are .64 in 1968 and .66 in 1971—not ideal, but reasonably satisfactory for research purposes. It therefore seems appropriate to treat the eleven items initially as a single set for detailed analysis, despite their somewhat heterogeneous content. But the limited homogeneity of the index, which is reenforced by our earlier finding that some items show change over time and some do not, requires us to pay continued attention to individual items as well as to summary scores. It should be noted that the merely moderate reliability of the index is due not only to the varied content of the items, but also to their varied format: this index lacks the uniform response set bias that contributes supriously to higher interitem correlations in many indices.

Exactly what to call this eleven-item index is more of a problem, especially since any such name easily comes to be hypostatized. As already remarked, some of the items might be thought of as measures of "militancy," some of "black consciousness," and some such as perceptions of job discrimination do not fit well under either rubric. Examination of the items one by one indicates that most of them involve distrust of, or dis-

---

[5]Scores 11 and 12 became 1; 13 and 14 became 2; . . . 31 and 32 became 11; there are no scores of 33 in either year. The pairs of categories collapsed always include one with only few cases because it results from missing data.

illusionment with, the actions of whites or white institutions (items 1, 2, 3, 4, 5, 6, 11) or preference for blacks or black institutions (7, 10). Only the two violence-related items (8, 9) do not fit these emphases directly, though they do fit indirectly as an indication of frustration over lack of change and they do correlate well with the total index. With these features in mind, we will refer to the index under the title *Alienation from White Society*, using the term *Alienation Index* for brevity. Because of the varied and vague uses of the concept "alienation" by social scientists, we should keep the full title in mind, and should recognize the special racial sense in which the concept "alienation" is employed here. Moreover, since the eleven items vary in the degree to which the term is appropriate and their intercorrelations are at best moderate, we will continue to refer back to, and often deal with, each of the separate items.

For analyses involving the Kerner-68 data we have only six of the eleven items available: items 1, 2, 3, 4, 7, and 8. Fortunately, these are among the better items both conceptually and methodologically, and we shall note later that they provide a reasonable substitute for the full index. The mean intercorrelation among the six items is .132, nearly the same as for the full DAS-68 set of eleven, although of course in index form the reliability is reduced because of fewer items. We shall refer to the six-item index below as the *Alienation Index* (*abb.*) to indicate its abbreviated size.[6] To assure ourselves that this shorter Kerner-68 index approximates in empirical meaning the full eleven-item index, we constructed the abbreviated version also for each of the DAS surveys, where it could be correlated with the full index. The correlations are .82 and .86 in DAS-68 and DAS-71, respectively, indicating that the abbreviated and full indexes are to a considerable degree interchangeable.

The Alienation Index Over Time

Our analysis now focuses on the Alienation Index as a single dependent variable. The comparison between mean scores in 1968 and 1971 serves to estimate the amount of change, as revealed by this index. In order to take account of factors that may disturb the comparison, or that may comprise

---

[6]Each item was scored on the same 3-point scale as in the two DAS surveys (footnote 1 above). Added together, an index is created that runs from 6 to 18 points; the highest two pairs of index categories (15 and 16, 17 and 18) were then collapsed because of small numbers of cases. Thus the final scale is 11 points in length (transformed to scores 1 to 11). Note that it is *not* directly comparable to the two 11-point DAS scales, since it is based on six rather than eleven items.

sources of change, we employ multiple classification analysis (MCA) as the primary technique for estimating change. The two studies, DAS-68 and DAS-71, constitute a two-category independent variable, and this variable, to be referred to as "Year," is used to predict scores on the Alienation Index. Other background variables are added as controls (predictors) in each MCA. At later points, Year will also be combined with certain of these controls to allow for possible interaction effects.

Scores on the Alienation Index are shown for each year in Table 3A for black interviewers only and in 3B for all interviewers. The increase in the index between 1968 and 1971 is, not unexpectedly, highly significant in

TABLE 3

Mean Scores on Alienation Index in 1968 and 1971 (with weighting)*

A. Black Interviewers Only

	Mean	Standard Deviation	Unweighted N	E^2	F	p	Mean, Adjusted for Sex
DAS-71	4.72	2.27	214				4.77
				1.7%	18.2	.001	
DAS-68	4.04	2.02	439				4.03
	0.68						0.74

B. All Interviewers

	Mean	Standard Deviation	Unweighted N	E^2	F	p	Mean, Adjusted for Sex and Race of Interviewer
DAS-71	4.35	2.24	342				4.45
				1.2%	13.8	.001	
DAS-68	3.85	2.01	600				3.81
	0.50						0.64

*DAS-68 is weighted for income stratum in both panels, and for the absence of the white interviewer sample in panel A. No weighting is needed for DAS-71. See Appendix A for explanation of weights. The between sum of squares d.f. is 1 in each panel.

TABLE 4

Mean Scores on Alienation Index in 1968 and 1971 (without weighting)

A. Black Interviewers Only

	Mean	Standard Deviation	N	E^2	F	p	Mean, Adjusted for Sex	Mean, Adjusted for Sex and Income
DAS-71	4.73	2.28	214	1.8%	11.8	.001	4.75	4.77
DAS-68	4.11 / 0.62	2.08	439				4.09 / 0.66	4.09 / 0.68

B. All Interviewers

	Mean	Standard Deviation	N	E^2	F	p	Mean, Adjusted for Interviewer	Mean, Adjusted for Sex, and Race-of-Interviewer	Mean, Adjusted for Sex, Race-of-Interviewer, and Income
DAS-71	4.36	2.24	342	1.1%	10.7	.01	4.42	4.45	4.46
DAS-68	3.89 / 0.47	2.06	600				3.85 / 0.57	3.84 / 0.61	3.83 / 0.63

both cases. (It is slightly larger when only the black interviewer samples are used, a point we will explore further below.) When sex of respondent and race-of-interviewer are controlled to take account of design variations in the two surveys (see Appendix A), the differences increase somewhat.

The DAS-68 data in Table 3 have been weighted to provide accurate representation of the Detroit population, as was done for the separate items in Table 1. However, this weighting affects the F statistics by inflating N's, and for most later purposes it would be useful to eliminate weighting. Table 4 presents these same data without weights, but with MCA controls for sex and family income. The addition of income serves to control those aspects of the DAS-68 sampling that are most closely connected to the need for weighting. Sex, and for the total sample, race-of-interviewer, are also included as controls to take account of the different assignment ratios for the two surveys (Appendix A). Comparison of Tables 3 and 4 indicates that for the black interviewer sample the absence of weighting decreases slightly the difference between the means by Year, a decrease which is not much affected by the addition of the income control. The F ratio declines appreciably, because of the reduced N, but remains highly significant. For the total sample, the lowered F now just misses the level needed for .001 significance, but otherwise the results are again not greatly affected by either the omission of weights or the addition of sex and income as controls. The use of race-of-interviewer as a control has somewhat more effect in moving the results closer to those produced by the properly weighted data. In sum, by tolerating a slight bias in our estimates of means we can eliminate weighting at most later points, thereby avoiding complications in analysis and significance testing. Inclusion of race-of-interviewer as a control is especially useful when dealing with the total samples and with Year as a predictor.

It is possible that there are other important variations in the demographic composition of the two Year samples. For example, the 21 to 29 year-old age category constitutes 25 percent of the 1968 sample, but only 15 percent of the 1971 sample. The consequences of such a difference depend on the relation of respondent's age to the Alienation Index, and the interpretation depends on whether the compositional difference involves real change or is due to sampling error. We will explore the relation of respondent's age and other specific variables to the Alienation Index below, but for the present it is useful to inquire whether the index differs by year once the two samples have been controlled on a number of major background variables. To this end, multiple classification analysis was carried out on the total unweighted sample with Year as a predictor, along with respondent's age, sex, education, and income, and race-of-interviewer as controls. The adjusted mean scores for 1968 and 1971 in this analysis are 3.84 and 4.45, respectively, yielding a difference (.61) approximately the same as that shown in the second panel of Table 3. Our basic conclusion that the Alienation Index shows a significant rise between 1968 and 1971 holds for all these analyses.

FIGURE 2

Distributions of Alienation Index Scores for DAS-68 and DAS-71 (Weighted as in Table 3)

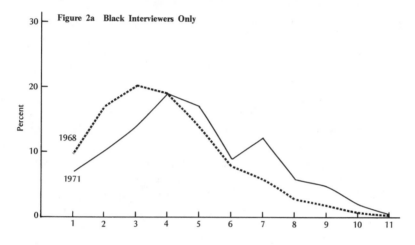

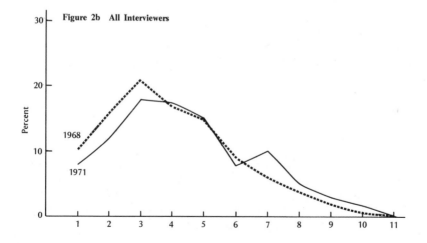

Figure 2 shows the complete Alienation Index distributions for the two years, with weighting still employed for the moment for exactness of representation. This figure allows visualization of where the mean change over time shown in Table 3 actually occurs in terms of the full distributions. The change shows up in shifts at both ends of the index: a smaller proportion of people are very low on the index in 1971 and a greater proportion are quite high. This was not inevitable, for the difference in means might have resulted entirely from shifts in the middle of the distribution or at one end only. Thus there tends to be movement toward relatively greater alienation from white society at all points of the 1968 distribution, both from those least alienated and from those most alienated at that earlier point.[7]

How large is the average shift from 1968 to 1971? One answer of course is that it is large enough to be statistically reliable with these sample sizes despite the briefness of the period measured. This surely gives it some importance, particularly if the same rate of change continues in future years. But it is less than one point (item) along our eleven-point scale, and less than half a standard deviation in scale scores in either year. Still another way of keeping the change in perspective is to note that the shift over time is *less* than that which occurs in either year when respondents shift from white to black interviewers. It is to this latter issue that we now turn.

---

[7]Throughout this analysis we assume that the population of Detroit has not been altered by mortality or migration over the three-year period in ways which would affect our results. We deal below (Chapter 5) with cohort changes.

4

EFFECTS OF RACE
OF INTERVIEWER

An earlier report on the DAS-68 survey demonstrated substantial differences between responses given to black and to white interviewers (Schuman and Converse, 1971). In general, black interviewers elicited answers indicating distrust of whites more frequently than did white interviewers. It is possible that *changes* in black attitudes between 1968 and 1971 also occurred more strongly for one race of interviewer than the other. This chapter investigates such a possibility, and deals at the same time with several other problems involving race-of-interviewer. As the earlier report emphasized, race-of-interviewer effects are important for substantive as well as methodological reasons, for interviewing itself is a microcosm of interaction. If blacks (or whites) offer different answers to black than to white interviewers, there is good reason to expect much the same variation in other forms of cross-racial communication.

Race-of-Interviewer Effects in the Separate Studies

Our first step is to repeat the basic race-of-interviewer findings for 1968—Schuman and Converse's report did not employ the Alienation Index used here—and then attempt to replicate the findings with the 1971 data. The main results of both these steps are presented in Table 5.

Panels A and B of Table 5 show highly reliable race-of-interviewer effects on Alienation Index scores for 1968. The first Panel (A) is for perfectly comparable subsamples only—where assignment by race-of-interviewer was random—and the second panel (B) is for the full 1968 probability

TABLE 5

Race-of-Interviewer Effects on Alienation Index Scores
in 1968 and 1971

A. 1968: DAS-68 Randomized Black and White Interviewer Samples Only*

	Mean	Standard Deviation	Unweighted N	E^2	F	p	Adjusted Means**
Black Interviewers	3.99	2.01	323				4.01
				3.1%	20.0	.001	
White Interviewers	3.25	1.86	161				3.23
	0.74						0.78

B. 1968: DAS-68 Complete Black and White Interviewer Samples*

	Mean	Standard Deviation	Unweighted N	E^2	F	p	Adjusted Means**
Black Interviewers	4.06	2.02	439				4.07
				3.1%	26.0	.001	
White Interviewers	3.24	1.86	161				3.21
	0.82						0.86

C. 1971: DAS-71 Complete Black and White Interviewer Samples

	Mean	Standard Deviation	Unweighted N	E^2	F	p	Adjusted Means**
Black Interviewers	4.73	2.27	214				4.74
				4.6%	16.3	.001	
White Interviewers	3.73	2.04	128				3.73
	1.00						1.01

*Panels A and B are weighted for income stratum only (see Appendix A). Panel C does not require weighting. Between sum of squares d.f. is 1 for each F ratio.
**Adjusted for sex and family income.

sample which included a non-randomized interviewer portion as well.[1] This difference in sample definition turns out to have negligible effects on results, and therefore in order to maximize sample size, later analysis

[1]The design of the 1968 interviewer experiment is described briefly in Appendix A. See also Schuman and Converse (1971) for further description and findings.

draws on the full 1968 sample that we have used in earlier chapters. Overall, we are able to explain approximately three percent of the variation in the Alienation Index by race-of-interviewer, not a large amount but comparable in size to that ordinarily contributed by "strong" background variables in attitude studies.[2]

The third panel (C) of Table 5 indicates that the 1971 data also show race-of-interviewer effects on the Alienation Index. The effects appear, if anything, somewhat greater in 1971 than in 1968, as measured both by the difference in means for black and white interviewers and by the magnitude of explained variation. A comparison of the total distribution of scores obtained by the two races of interviewers in 1971 reveals shifts along the entire scale.

Some individual items do show considerable variation in interviewer effects from one year to the other, as indicated in Table 6. In 1968, Question 3 (Trust) revealed the largest interviewer effect of the eleven in the index ($E^2 = 9.4$ percent), but in 1971 the effect was considerably reduced ($E^2 = 2.2$ percent).[3] On the other hand, the largest effect in 1971 was for Question 2 (Keep Down), $E^2 = 8.6$ percent, while in 1968 that item showed an explained variation of only 1.0 percent. These are probably regression phenomena, and suggest that it is a mistake to focus too single-mindedly on any one item. The important point to note is that *both* of the two items just mentioned are concerned with negative beliefs about whites; thus the changes in magnitude of effect do not challenge the more basic interpretation advanced by Schuman and Converse, that it is in this sphere especially—and understandably—that blacks give different responses to white and black interviewers. Moreover, the Spearman rank-order correlation across all eleven items in terms of variation explained in 1968 and 1971 is substantial (rho = .51): the same items tend to show relatively strong effects in both years.

---

[2]This effect is much less strong, however, than the 16.6 percent reported by Schuman and Converse (1971). For that earlier analysis a scale was deliberately constructed from items initially found to have race-of-interviewer effects. This procedure obviously inflated the interviewer effect for the final scale, partly by defining it in a real but purely empirical way and probably partly by capitalizing on chance variations among items. The lower degree of association indicated here for the Alienation Index is more generalizable to other broad sets of similar racial questions that might be asked of blacks, since the eleven items we began with in Chapter 1 had been selected for replication on the basis of representative content, not interviewer effects.

[3]These E^2's differ slightly from those reported by Schuman and Converse (1971) because of differences in sample definition.

TABLE 6

Associations Between Race-of-Interviewer
and Items in 1968 and 1971*

Item Number and Identification		Percent Variation Explained (E^2)	
		DAS-68	DAS-71
1	Progress	0.1	0.2
2	Keep down	1.0	8.6
3	Trust	9.4	2.2
4	Clerks	2.0	2.7
5	Jobs	0.0	0.4
6	Teachers	2.7	0.3
7	Neighborhood	1.8	0.9
8	Best means	0.0	0.0
9	Second means	0.0	1.5
10	Principals	2.5	0.6
11	Fight for U.S.	0.0	0.1

*See Table 1 for complete wording. Items have been dichotomized for the present calculations. Minimum unweighted N's are 516 for DAS-68 and 294 for DAS-71. The DAS-68 data are weighted by income strata (see Appendix A). All items in this table show higher (more alienated) scores for black interviewers, with the exception of item 5 (Jobs) where a slight and non-significant reversal occurs.

Race-of-Interviewer and Attitude Change

Although race-of-interviewer effects are significant in both 1968 and 1971, they appear to be somewhat greater in the later year. Put another way and in the form of a query, is it the case that there is greater change in black attitudes over the 1968-71 period for interviews conducted by blacks than for those conducted by whites?

Statistically, this becomes a question of whether Year and race-of-interviewer interact in their effects on Alienation Index scores. Using multiple classification analysis, the effects of such an interaction, represented by a combined Year-Interviewer variable, are compared in Table 7 with the additive effects of the two variables entered as separate predictors. The analysis provides little evidence for such interaction, Despite the apparent trend for the 1968-71 difference to be greater for black than for white interviewers (the difference in Alienation means for blacks is .72; for whites, .45). the scores produced by simply *adding* the effects of the two separate variables are within 0.1 of the actual scores for the four Year-by-Interviewer categories. The improvement in explained sum of squares by allowing for interaction is less than 0.1% and does not approach significance. Thus the slight trend for change to be greater among black interviewers can best be treated as due to sampling error.[4] If it represents a real trend over time, its effects are still too small to be demonstrated at the present time.

TABLE 7

Effects of Year and Race-of-Interviewer on Alienation Index Scores*

Combined Year-Interviewer Categories	N	Additive Model	Actual Means
Black-71	202	4.67	4.70
White-71	122	3.67	3.57
Black-68	410	4.01	3.98
White-68	155	3.04	3.12

*All means have been adjusted for sex and income effects, the first because the two samples differ in proportions of men and women, the second as a means of controlling for disproportionate sampling of income strata in DAS-68 (see Appendix A). No weighting has been used.

Race-of-interviewer and Year thus constitute independent predictors of black racial attitudes. (In this study they are slightly correlated because the proportions of black and white interviewers differed a bit in the two years, but we have generally removed this "accidental" correlation

[4]Or to the slight age-of-interviewer effects to be discussed below. DAS-68 was administered by older black and younger white interviewers, while DAS-71 included all four age-race combinations. The addition of younger blacks and older whites to the black and white interviewer groups increases the difference in scores between them. If only older black and younger white interviewers are considered in 1971, E^2 for race-of-interviewer is reduced from 4.6 percent to 2.6 percent.

through multiple classification analysis.) Figure 3 compares the effects of change in Alienation scores over time for the total sample with the change in scores that occurs when respondents shift from black to white interviewers. We can see that for this three year period, race-of-interviewer is at least as important a factor in black racial attitudes as is the change over time. Of course, over a longer period this would very likely cease to be true.

FIGURE 3

**A Comparison of Alienation Index Scores by Year (1968 and 1971)
and by Race-of-Interviewer
(Black and White Interviewer Samples for Both 1968 and 1971)***

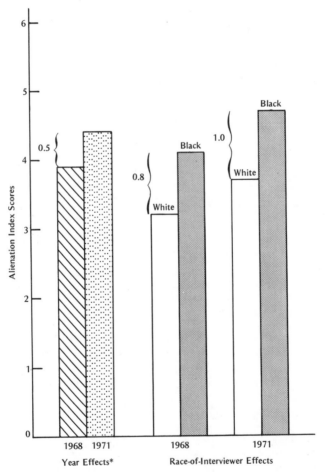

*Based on Total Interviewer Samples for DAS-68 and DAS-71 each year.

Age of Interviewer

The earlier DAS-68 study was not able to separate race-of-interviewer effects from possible age and organizational differences among interviewers. Black interviewers in the 1968 survey were primarily older professional Survey Research Center interviewers, while the white interviewers were generally younger Sociology graduate students. The DAS-71 design does, however, allow us to distinguish effects of race-of-interviewer from the age-organizational factor, although the latter two characteristics overlap too greatly for adequate separation. On the assumption that age is the more important variable, we focus on age-of-interviewer and divide the 1971 sample into "over 30" vs. "30 and under." [5]

The general hypothesis to be investigated is that black respondents will assume or perceive younger black interviewers to be more militant than older black interviewers, and will respond to this attribution with greater militancy themselves. Similarly, although less compelling, young white interviewers will be assumed or perceived to be more liberal in racial attitudes than older white interviewers, and this attribution again will lead to greater militancy of response by black respondents. We have no way of testing directly the assumptions and perceptions that respondents hold about interviewers, but we can determine whether levels of respondent militancy, as measured by the Alienation Index, vary systematically with age-of-interviewer.

The hypothesis, if confirmed, has two very important implications for the results reported in this volume. One concerns the validity of black attitude responses; the other, our interpretation of change between 1968 and 1971. First, if age-of-interviewer effects do occur, this suggests that black responses on racial issues are easily swayed by desires to conform to the assumed views of interviewers. If this is true for age-of-interviewer, it may well be true for race-of-interviewer also. The latter effects have usually been interpreted to mean that blacks give more *valid* responses to black interviewers—thus the common practice in recent surveys of matching interviewer and respondent by race—but the effects might be no more than an indication that black responses are not stable and simply conform to whatever are thought to be the wishes of interviewers. Race-of-inter-

---

[5]This cutting point not only has theoretical merit in terms of the likely perceptions by respondents of "young" and "older" interviewers, but also reflects a natural break in the age distribution for our interviewers. Of the 64 interviewers, 28 were within the age range 22 to 30, only three within the range 31 to 35, and the rest over 35 (all but five beyond 40). Most of the 30-and-under interviewers were Detroit Area Study graduate students; most of those over-30 were Survey Research Center professionals.

viewer effects, such as those reported in Table 5, and earlier by Hyman (1954), Williams (1968), and Schuman and Converse (1971), would point not so much to greater openness of black respondents to black interviewers, but rather to a lack of firm attitudes altogether. [6]

A second implication of age-of-interviewer effects would be of less general import, but bears directly on our conclusions from Tables 1 and 3 about attitude change between 1968 and 1971. The black interviewing staff for DAS-68 was composed almost entirely of "older" interviewers, while the black interviewing staff for DAS-71 included about one third "younger" interviewers. If young interviewers per se elicit more militant responses than older interviewers, then the rise in apparent Alienation between the two dates could be due simply to the differences in staff composition in the two years. In sum, age-of-interviewer effects are of critical importance to our investigation of both the degree of attitude change and the validity of attitude measurement among black respondents.

Table 8 presents DAS-71 estimates of age-of-interviewer and race-of-interviewer effects separately, additively, and in interaction. The effect of race-of-interviewer, already large ($E^2 = 4.6$ percent), increases slightly (to 5.1 percent) when age-of interviewer is controlled. [7] The gross effect of age-of-interviewer is essentially zero, but controlling for race-of-interviewer raises it slightly from 0.1 percent to 0.5 percent—still only half of one percent in explained variation. The F ratio for this increment is 1.66 (1,338 df), which fails to reach significance at the .05 level.

It is possible that age- and race-of-interviewer interact, for example, that it is only among black interviewers that age makes a difference, while whites are perceived alike irrespective of age. The bottom half of Table 6 presents age- and race-of-interviewer in combination, and indicates that this is not the case. The large and significant race-of-interviewer effects *added* to the smaller and non-significant age-of-interviewer effects reproduce well the means actually obtained for each age-race combination. Although the ordering of the four means is intuitively compelling, in fact the age component may easily be due to chance. If there is a true age effect, it is too tiny to be detected reliably with a sample of this size, nor

---

[6]The hypothesis in this form was first developed by Quarm (1971).

[7]This is because age-of-interviewer and race-of-interviewer are negatively related, as can be seen from the N's when the two are combined in the lower panel of Table 8. This is not a "finding," of course, but simply a result of the distribution on age- and race-of-interviewer available to us for field work in 1971.

TABLE 8

Effects of Race- and Age-of-Interviewer on Alienation Index Scores (DAS-71)

A. Race- and Age-of-Interviewer as Separate Predictors:

Race of Interviewer	N	Mean	Explained Sum of Squares (E^2)	Adjusted Mean*	Explained Sum of Squares
Black Interviewers	214	4.73		4.76	
			4.6%		5.1%
White Interviewers	128	3.73		3.68	
		1.00		1.08	
Age of Interviewer					
Young Interviewers	162	4.38		4.53	
			0.0%		0.5%
Older Interviewers	180	4.33		4.21	
		0.05		0.32	

B. Combined Race-Age of Interviewer

	N	Actual Means**	Explained Sum of Squares	Additive Model***	Explained Sum of Squares
Young-Black	80	4.87		4.93	
Older-Black	134	4.64		4.61	
			5.2%		5.1%
Young-White	82	3.90		3.84	
Older-White	46	3.42		3.52	

*Each predictor is controlled for the other through MCA, with sex included as a third predictor for control purposes.

**Combined categories are treated as a single variable in MCA, with sex included as a second predictor for control purposes.

***Calculated by adding to the grand mean the net effect for the appropriate age category and the net effect for the appropriate race category.

can it be of much practical importance.[8] Note also that insofar as there is any evidence of interaction, it is among white rather than black interviewers (the difference between the means is .48 in the one case, .23 in the other)—which does not fit well the original hypothesis which emphasized young black interviewers being perceived as especially militant and thereby eliciting more militant responses.

A similar analysis was carried out for item 2 in Table 1. Since this item is one showing a particularly large change over time, it is useful for determining whether the results in Table 1 could be seriously biased by age-of-interviewer effects. The percentage saying "keep down" for each age-race category of interviewer in DAS-71 is as follows (with respondent's sex controlled):

	N	Percentage responding "keep down"
Young black	80	45.0
Older black	132	39.4
Young white	76	14.5
Older white	45	11.1

As with the overall Alienation Index there are slight trends here for age-of-interviewer to make a difference: 5.6 percent among black interviewers and 3.4 percent among white. But the difference of 24.9 percent between older black and young white interviewers dwarfs either of these, indicating that race-of-interviewer is far more important than age-of-interviewer. Furthermore, if we substitute the older black figure of 39.4 percent for the DAS-71 percentage of 40.9 percent on this item in table 1—thus holding age constant between the two years—we still obtain a difference of 16.7 percent ($\chi^2 = 18.9$, 1 d.f., $p < .001$) between 1968 and 1971. This is only slightly smaller than the 18.2 percent difference shown in Table 1.

In sum, the 1968-1971 changes do not seem to be due to differences in age-of-interviewer to any important degree. And the importance of race-of-interviewer effects, as against the unimportance of age-of-interviewer effects, leaves intact the interpretation that differences by race-of-interviewer signify lesser validity for interviews gathered by whites.

---

[8]The order of means in Table 8 is what would be predicted on the assumption of both race- and age-of interviewer effects, assuming the former to be the stronger. Since there are (4 x 3 x 2 x 1) permutations, the probability of any single one occurring is 1 out of 24, or less than .05. Thus there is some basis in terms of conventional significance levels for regarding the order as not due to chance. There is also, of course, the possibility that age-of-interviewer takes on more importance in certain special interactions, for example, with age of respondent.

Race-of-Interviewer Effects on Non-Racial Items

Our primary concern in this chapter is with the effect of race-of-interviewer on the items that make up the Alienation Index, and more generally on racial attitude questions asked of blacks. But the DAS-71 questionnaire, together with the randomized assignment of interviewers by race, provides an unusual opportunity to determine the extent to which this interviewer characteristic affects black responses on *non*-racial attitude items as well.[9] We digress briefly to touch on this issue.

The DAS-71 questionnaire consisted of a wide range of items from a number of earlier surveys, repeated in 1971 for the purpose of studying social change across many areas of life (Duncan, Schuman, and Duncan, 1973). From the total set of (non-racial) items, we first selected for broad coverage ten closed questions, and cross-tabulated them with race-of-interviewer. Nine showed no difference approaching significance, but a question on whether the "Star-Spangled Banner" should be replaced as the national anthem exhibited a highly significant interviewer effect (see Table 9, item a). The finding suggested that such effects might occur especially on questions dealing with conventional patriotic themes. Twenty additional items were then analyzed, and politically related items again tended to show significant or near-significant interviewer differences (see items b, c, d, e, and f in Table 9)—in each case with the politically more conservative response given to white interviewers. This replication over several political items, plus the fact that there are no interviewer effects at all on a wide range of non-political items (e.g., whether there is a life after death, whether boys and girls should have different household chores, whether physicians do a good job, whether children should learn mainly obedience or mainly independent thinking), points to the area of political allegiance as specifically sensitive to race-of-interviewer. It is not difficult to see how such non-racial political items might become charged with racial connotations for black respondents, and thus lead to differential answers according to the race of the inquirer.

We also found that another type of non-racial item showed significant interviewer effects: agree-disagree statements (g and h in Table 9) similar in format to items noted in past research on agreeing response set (Lenski and Leggett, 1960; Carr, 1971). However, the two non-political items presented in Table 9 are the only ones out of some dozen such agree-disagree non-political items to reveal such effects. Differences on the

---

[9]Schuman and Converse (1971) concluded that race-of-interviewer effects were uncommon and often uninterpretable on non-racial items, but their data did not include many non-racial *attitude* items.

TABLE 9

Race-of-Interviewer Effects on Non-Racial Attitude Items (DAS-71)

Item and Key Response	Black Interviewers	White Interviewers	χ^2(1 d.f.)	p
a. *"Many people find the Star-Spangled Banner difficult to sing. If a new and appropriate national anthem were written, would you object to substituting it for the Star-Spangled Banner?"* **No**	77%	58%	13.1	.001
b. *"Which of these two statements do you agree with most? (1) The Founding Fathers had so much wisdom that our constitution handles most modern problems very well; (2) While the Founding Fathers were very wise, the Constitution they wrote needs frequent changes to bring it up to date."* **Needs frequent changes**	91%	77%	11.1	.001
c. *"Are you well satisfied, more or less satisfied, or not at all satisfied with the protection provided for your neighborhood by the police?"* **More or less and not at all**	85%	74%	5.1	.05
d. *"In our country, the Constitution guarantees the right of free speech to everyone. In your opinion, does this include the right for someone to make speeches criticizing what the president does?"* **Yes**	83%	74%	3.1	.10
e. *"Public officials really care about what people like me think."* **Agree**	35%	46%	4.3	.05
f. *"Every American family should be required by law to own a flag."* **Agree**	18%	37%	4.3	.05
g. *"Given enough time and money, almost all of man's important problems can be solved by science."* **Agree**	25%	45%	14.0	.001
h. *"It's hardly fair to bring children into the world the way things look for the future."* **Agree**	39%	56%	11.4	.001

others do not approach significance, and indeed four such items produce higher agreement to black interviewers than to white. Thus it is clearly too simple to say that black respondents tend to "agree" more with general statements of the anomie type when they are offered by white than by black interviewers. We are uncertain as to what interpretation to give to these relatively isolated agree-disagree effects, but they appear to be too reliable to attribute simply to chance.

Thus, we have discovered two different types of non-racial attitude items susceptible to race-of-interviewer effects: those bearing on allegiance to the polity and certain still difficult to specify agree-disagree statements. For practical survey research purposes both types deserve note, but for theoretical purposes it is the political questions that seem most relevant. As with the entertainer item discussed earlier (Chapter 2), these political items show that responses may be influenced on certain types of non-racial survey questions in the same way that they are on questions about overtly racial issues. When black and white *respondents* are to be compared in terms of political attitudes, race-of-interviewer may be an important variable requiring control. [10]

Conclusions and a Remaining Problem

We have shown that race-of-interviewer is an important determinant of certain black racial attitudes, and indeed of some non-racial attitudes as well. These interviewer effects are somewhat greater in magnitude than the change in attitude level between 1968 and 1971 when race-of-interviewer is held constant. However, race-of-interviewer does not appear to interact with attitude change over time, and thus in arriving at inferences about rates of attitude change either race of interviewer may be used, provided it is held constant. It would be misleading to compare responses obtained in earlier years by all-white interviewing staffs with responses obtained today by black interviewers. Race-of-interviewer will also, of course, affect one's reports of absolute response levels: on sensitive items the results obtained by black and white interviewers can differ by as much as 25 percent (see Schuman and Converse, 1971, for specific examples).

---

[10]One political item (on freedom of speech for Communists) does not show a race-of-interviewer effect—for reasons not clear to us. Moreover, several of the political items in Table 9 are rather long and awkward in wording, and this may well contribute to the interviewer effect. Thus our conclusions even here cannot be completely straightforward, and further efforts at both data-gathering and conceptualization are needed to understand adequately the special character of race-of-interviewer effects on non-racial attitude items.

It is usually assumed that race-of-interviewer effects point to greater validity of responses given to black interviewers. We have provided further evidence that this is the case by showing that age-of-interviewer has little or no effect on response. Thus it is not the case that black respondents are affected by all characteristics of interviewers; rather, it is the race of the interviewer that seems especially important. It may also be noted that we have shown elsewhere (Hatchett and Schuman, 1974) quite large effects on white responses when race-of-interviewer is introduced as a variable. Both these findings seem to fit best the common sense assumption that on racial matters persons are simply more frank with members of what they perceive to be their own race. Let us add, however, that this does not mean that cross-racial responses are unimportant. As was remarked in an earlier study:

> . . .there is a type of valid insight that "white effects" in survey interviewing may provide. If white interviewers serve to depress the "natural" level of militancy of black respondents, we must expect something similar to happen in other white-black interaction outside the survey context, for example, in ordinary integrated social situations. Moreover, as caste breaks down in this country, the presence of blacks in social situations no doubt tends to have a similar effect on whites, namely, to decrease open expression of anti-black sentiments. Thus integrated social situations, like "integrated interviewing situations," should inhibit overt hostility on both sides. While this may lead to some underestimation of latent negative feelings, it may also reduce interracial provocations and therefore decrease some of the areas of friction between blacks and whites (Schuman and Converse, 1971).

There is one important remaining problem involving race-of-interviewer. It is possible that *relationships* between black attitudes and other variables differ depending upon whether interviewers are black or white. Indeed, Schuman and Converse (1971) report just such a trend with regard to income and education:

> . . .An analyst examining the data collected only by *white interviewers* would find militancy scores positively related to social status, and would conclude that as blacks become better educated and attain higher incomes they are likely to become more militant. With *black interviewers,* however, there is no clear systematic variation in mean militancy scores by respondent's status. Hence an analyst examining such data would conclude that militancy is spread fairly evenly over the black social class structure and is not a function of such factors as low economic status at the one extreme or high education at the other.

Since this problem involves the demographic and socioeconomic correlates of the Alienation Index, we reserve treatment of it for the next chapter.

5

DEMOGRAPHIC AND SOCIOECONOMIC FACTORS

Just as attitude change between 1968 and 1971 could have occurred in interaction with race-of-interviewer, so interaction of change with major demographic and socioeconomic variables can readily be imagined. Looked at one way, there is the issue of whether sex, for example, is similarly related to the Alienation Index in both years; from a complimentary standpoint the issue is whether change between the two years occurred to the same extent for men and for women. These questions are analytically the same, for they both ask whether sex, time difference, and attitudinal response interact and if so, in what way. If significant interaction with Year is *not* present, we can usefully collapse the two Year samples in order to obtain a better estimate of the relationship between particular background factors and attitude. We shall be fairly liberal in noting nonsignificant interaction trends, since even genuine interactions of this type are likely to be small for the limited time period involved, and thus difficult to detect with our sample sizes.[1]

Sex

Alienation Index means by sex and year are presented in Table 10. Men have higher scores than women in both years, and 1971 scores for both sexes are higher than 1968 scores. Although the difference in means

---

[1]Except as specifically noted in this chapter, 1968 refers to DAS-68 and 1971 to DAS-71 data.

between men and women is smaller in 1971 (.26) than in 1968 (.59), the interaction effect is trivial (0.1 percent increment in explained variation) and non-significant (F = 1.41, d.f. = 1; 927).[2] When the two Year samples are aggregated, sex explains 1.1 percent of the total variation above that explained by Year and the other variables noted in Table 10. This increment is easily significant (F = 11.68, d.f. = 1; 930, p < .001) despite its modest size. The effect of sex obviously draws heavily on the larger difference and larger sample size from 1968, and leaves us with some uncertainty about the role of sex differences in future responses to questions of the type under consideration here. If only the 1971 sample had been available, we could not have rejected the null hypothesis of no sex difference (F = 0.74, d.f. = 1; 341). For now we must regard this lack of significance as due to sampling error, but conceivably it represents the beginning of a trend toward reduction or elimination of the attitude difference between men and women found in the 1968 data.

Examination of three individual items (numbers 2, 7, and 8 from Table 1) above also fails to show any reliable changes in sex difference over time. The test for interaction employs Goodman's procedure (1970; Davis, 1974)

---

[2]It may be useful to detail the procedure followed in this and later tests. All four of the means in Table 10 are subject to sampling error, and therefore the apparently greater 1968-1971 increase for women than for men may result from such random error. Multiple classification analysis is used to estimate the four means on the assumption of simple addition of separate sex and Year effects. The expected mean for each sex-Year combination is the grand mean of all four subsamples combined (4.058 in this case), plus the net effects for a given category of sex and of Year. (Net effects through MCA are used to control for any correlation between Year and sex, which in this instance is slight. In addition, in this analysis race-of-interviewer, income, and age were included as controls.) For example, the net increment to respondents for being in the 1971 sample is +.359 and the net effect for being female is -.233; hence the expected mean for women in 1971 is: 4.058 + .359 - .233 = 4.184. This and the other three means expected on the basis of additivity are shown in the last column of Table 10. Comparison of these additive means with the actual means in column 2 reveals differences that may be a result of interaction between Year and sex. It will be observed that the differences between the columns 2 and 3 are not as great as the differences referred to earlier—a consequence of the fact that the additive model is based on deviations from the average for sex for both years and for Year for both sexes.

The proportion of variation in Alienation Index scores explained by the additive model in this case is 11.39 percent. When interaction between sex and Year is allowed, the explained variation increases to 11.537—an increment of only about one-tenth of a percent. The additive model has 13 degrees of freedom, the interaction model 14, hence the increment in explained sum of squares involves 1 degree of freedom. An F test for this increment, as noted in the text, does not approach significance. Thus we conclude that sampling error could readily account for the apparent differential change by sex between 1968 and 1971.

TABLE 10

Alienation Index Scores by Sex and Year (DAS-68 and DAS-71)

Sex and Year	N	Actual Means*	Additive Model*
Males-71	140	4.53	4.66
Females-71	202	4.27	4.18
Males-68	321	4.15	4.10
Females-68	279	3.56	3.63
	942		

*Adjusted for race-of-interviewer, respondent's age, respondent's income.

for constructing a model allowing associations between each pair of variables but no three-way interaction. The adequacy of the model is then tested against the observed data, using the likelihood-ratio chi square statistic. Such a two-variable model fits easily for each of the three Alienation items, hence we reject the hypothesis of three-way interaction among sex, Year, and item. Indeed, the three items do not even agree in directions of trend, which reenforces our caution about asserting any change over time in the relation of sex to the Alienation items.

TABLE 11

Alienation Index Scores by Age and Year*

Age Category	N	DAS-68 Mean Score	N	DAS-71 Mean Score	N	Combined Years Mean Score
21-29	96	4.52	87	5.57	183	4.94
30-39	157	4.01	73	4.54	230	4.21
40-49	175	3.84	81	3.86	256	3.88
50-59	106	3.28	65	4.01	171	3.56
60-69	66	3.06	35	4.15	101	3.45

*Means adjusted for sex, education, income, Year, and race-of-interviewer by multiple classification analysis.

Age

Age has appeared to be the strongest "background" correlate of black racial attitudes in most, if not all, recent studies: younger black respondents tend to answer questions in a more militant and separatist direction (Murphy and Watson, 1970; Caplan and Paige, 1968; Campbell and Schuman, 1968; Edwards, 1972; Caplan, 1970). Table 11 shows this same age relationship to exist for the more general Alienation Index in 1968, and to persist in 1971. In the 1968 data the relationship is consistently monotonic; in 1971 the 21-29 year-olds have distinctively high scores, but beyond the age of 40 the relationship is flat and, if anything, reversed in direction. Interaction between age and Year reaches only borderline significance (F = 2.09, d.f. = 4; 919, p < .10), hence we must regard the difference between the two Year distributions as probably due to sampling error.[3] We are left with strong evidence of the continued gap between the views of younger and older blacks, but some uncertainty about whether the age groups show a meaningful difference beyond the 30 to 39 year age category.

If the two Year samples are aggregated, the variation in Alienation scores explained by age beyond that explained by other background factors noted in Table 11 is 4.4 percent (F = 10.96, d.f. = 4; 919, p < .001), and one and a half points on the Alienation Index separate the youngest and oldest age-by-decade categories. If the two years are treated separately, the variation explained by age actually increases in 1971 over that in 1968, despite the flattening of the later age groups.[4] Analysis of the combined Year samples separately by sex (not shown) indicates a similar degree of association between the index and age for men and women.

Since the youngest age category, 21-29, appears to be a critical one both in its mean score relative to the rest of the sample and in its apparent rate of change over the three-year period, it deserves closer investigation. In particular, we would like to know to what extent these differences represent attitude change within a fixed population and to what extent changes in the composition of that population are involved. The 21-29 sub-population in 1968 was 24-32 years old by 1971, and thus the new 21-29 category

---

[3]Examination of five separate index items reveals four non-significant interactions between age and time, and one that is barely significant but unclear in direction. It appears reasonable to regard the basic age pattern as persisting over the two years, as was done for the Index as a whole, and to examine the relationship between age and each item for the combined samples.

[4]In 1968, E^2 = 3.1 percent; in 1971, E^2 = 7.6 percent. These are without controls.

consisted partly of those who had been 18-20 at the time of the earlier survey and were therefore not interviewed. The time period is too short and our 1971 sample too small to allow cohort analysis here that is more than suggestive, but steps in that direction are taken in Table 12. Since the DAS-68 and DAS-71 surveys began at almost exactly the same point in the calendar year, and extended for about the same period, we define cohorts in terms of age at last birthday in each study. Table 12 shows the new cohort in 1971—those who were 18-20 in 1968 and 21-23 in 1971—with the highest mean score, suggesting that some of the evidence of change we have discovered is a result of change in population composition. Since only a very small proportion of our 1971 sample comes from this alteration of the population, however, replacement can be only one factor in the 1968-1971 difference. On the other hand, evidence in the table for intra-cohort attitude shifting is more mixed, no doubt in part because of the large amount of sampling error attached to these tiny cohort samples.

TABLE 12

Alienation Index Scores by Selected Three-Year Cohorts*

Cohort (Age in 1968)		Age in 1971		Mean Alienation Scores* 1968	1971
	N		N		
(18-20)	—	21-23	(26)	(not in-terviewed)	5.64
21-23	(19)	24-26	(38)	5.12	5.22
24-26	(39)	27-29	(23)	4.68	5.40
27-29	(38)	30-32	(25)	4.19	4.09

*Means adjusted for sex, education, income, and race-of-interviewer.

A more reliable comparison of a single grand cohort over time is afforded by restricting ouselves to those 21 to 66 in 1968 and 24 to 69 in 1971. The adjusted means for this single massive cohort are 3.87 in 1968 and 4.37 in 1971, which can be compared with the total sample means in Table 4 reported earlier.[5] Of the original difference of 0.63 between the two

---

[5]In both analyses, Year is used as a MCA predictor, along with sex, income, and race-of-interviewer.

years, a crude estimate is that four-fifths is accounted for by intracohort attitude change and the remaining one-fifth by the addition of the 18-21 category from 1968 and the loss of the 67-69 category from the same year. The bulk of the difference is thus attributed to intracohort attitude change, but a surprisingly large proportion to the three-year categories at either end of our age scale. Of course, the latter may have also shown attitude change over the same period, and thus we probably overestimate the pure replacement contribution somewhat.

Education and Age

The relationship between education and black racial attitudes has been much less clear in recent studies than is the case for age. Gary Marx (1967) found a positive association between education and conventional civil rights attitudes in the mid-sixties, but the several post-riot studies report little or no relationship when more contemporary militancy is involved (Schuman, 1972b).

Table 13 reveals an interesting curvilinear pattern of association for the Alienation Index in both 1968 and 1971. College graduates have the highest scores, followed by those with the least number of years of schooling completed. Relatively low scores are found among those with high school degrees or some college. (There is no sign of interaction between education and Year: $F = 0.88$, d.f. $= 4$; 925, n.s. When the two Year samples are aggregated, education accounts for 1.4 percent of the variation in the index [$F = 6.88$, d.f. $= 4$; 929 $p < .001$].)

Table 13 is based on the entire age range in our sample, with age and sex controlled, but further analysis reveals the curvilinearity in Alienation scores to be located among younger respondents only, as shown in Table 14. For this analysis, age (21-35, 36-49, 50+) and education (0-11, 12, 13+ years of school) were included as separate predictors, and again as a combined single predictor in a multiple classification analysis—the latter scores being shown in Table 14. With year, sex, and race-of-interviewer controlled, the increment in explained variation due to the age-education interaction is significant at the .05 level ($F = 2.53$, d.f. $= 4$; 929). The curvilinear relationship in Alienation scores is clearly visible within the 21-35 age group in Table 14, but disappears completely in the older age categories, the oldest showing no trend at all. The age relationship previously described—younger persons having higher scores—appears at each educational level, but is stronger at the two ends of the educational hierarchy. Thus alienation from white society seems to emerge most strongly among

TABLE 13

Alienation Index Scores by Education for DAS-68, DAS-71, and Combined Years*

Completed years of education	DAS-68			DAS-71			Combined 1968 and 1971		
	N	Mean	Adjusted Mean	N	Mean	Adjusted Mean	N	Mean	Adjusted Mean
0-8	143	3.68	3.96	69	4.28	4.66	212	3.87	4.21
9-11	178	3.93	3.89	97	4.55	4.64	275	4.15	4.16
12	174	3.89	3.75	116	4.13	3.94	290	3.99	3.81
13-15	64	3.69	3.51	42	4.39	4.29	106	3.97	3.80
16+	41	4.74	4.51	17	5.15	5.32	58	4.86	4.80

*All means are adjusted for sex, age, and race-of-interviewer. Combined 1968 and 1971 means are also adjusted for Year.

the *least* and the *most* educated sections of the younger black population.[6] The reasons may be different at the two ends of the educational ladder, but an implicit alliance of sentiment between the new black intellectual elite and those furthest removed from the educational mainstream can be envisaged.

TABLE 14

Mean Alienation Index Scores by Education and Age*

Completed years of education	Ages 21-35		Ages 36-49		Ages 50-69	
0-11	4.88	(106)	4.02	(183)	3.59	(198)
12	4.11	(145)	3.99	(102)	3.60	(43)
13+	5.08	(69)	3.77	(64)	3.56	(31)

*Combined DAS-68 and DAS-71 samples. Means are adjusted for Year, sex, and race-of-interviewer. N's are shown in parentheses.

A Complication: Race-of-Interviewer

In the previous chapter we noted the possibility that interviewer's race might affect relationships between the Alienation Index and various background factors. This was not the case for sex or age, and the findings presented in Tables 10 and 11 hold up well when the analysis is carried out separately for black and white interviewers. But the results just discussed for education appear to differ by race-of-interviewer: Table 15 shows that the curvilinear association prevails only for the data for black interviewers, while for white interviewers there is little relationship of any kind except that the small college group has distinctively high scores. Looked at another way that is easier to interpret, those with college education answer similarly to black and white interviewers, but those with lesser education produce higher Alienation scores when the interviewer is black.

The increment due to interaction effects between education and race-of-interviewer on Alienation scores reaches borderline significance ($F = 3.04$, d.f. $= 2$; 811, $p < .05$) but the small number of cases at the college graduate level warns against regarding the exact shapes of the relationships in Table 15 as reliable. We cannot test further the shape of the

[6]When sex is controlled, the curvilinear relationship holds for both men and women, though more strongly for men.

TABLE 15

Alienation Index Scores by Education and Race-of-Interviewer*

Completed years of education	Black Interviewers		White Interviewers	
	Mean	N	Mean	N
0-8	4.49	(124)	3.37	(63)
9-11	4.55	(152)	3.49	(87)
12	4.15	(158)	3.17	(93)
13-15	3.81	(68)	3.72	(27)
16+	4.75	(35)	4.76	(18)

*DAS-68 and DAS-71 combined. Sex and age are controlled through multiple classification analysis.

relationship for white interviewers, but in the earlier Kerner-68 study we have a large sample interviewed only by black interviewers. Table 16 shows that for all 15 cities sampled in Kerner-68, a similar curvilinear relationship holds among younger blacks (21-35) on the abbreviated six-item version of the Alienation Index.[7] The college level and grade school level sam-

TABLE 16

Alienation Index Scores by Education for Kerner-68 Study*

Completed years of education	N	Mean**
0-8	57	5.18
9-11	279	4.75
12	311	4.33
13-15	103	4.12
16+	32	4.46

*Respondents ages 21-35, black interviewers only.
**Adjusted by multiple classification analysis for sex and age (21-25, 26-30, 31-35).

---

[7]However, the highest means are at the lower educational end rather than the college end. Note that exact scores are not directly comparable to the DAS tables, since the Kerner-68 index is based on fewer items.

ples are again small, but there is the same trend for Alienation scores to be high among the *least educated* and the *most educated* younger people. The addition of education to the multiple classification analysis, over and above age and sex, explains 1.4 percent of the variation in scores and is significant at the .05 level (F = 2.62, d.f. = 4; 778). Note that in this analysis age has been controlled within the 21-35 age range in order to prevent spurious effects. There is no association between education and Alienation among older blacks (data not shown).

Complex relationships of this type are more uncertain in reliability and interpretation than simple monotonic ones—and replication is certainly essential—but the present finding shows enough stability to be worth some stress as a problem for further investigation. The fact that it occurs only among younger blacks suggests that these are emerging trends. It is tempting to see the two educational extremes as experiencing in different ways the frustrations of blacks in America: the least educated "drop-out" group exposed to street realities and cynicism, the college graduates to more ideological shifts in black consciousness. In between one would find the black equivalents of Middle America, less alienated from white society and perhaps more eager to become part of it.

Age, Education, and Individual Items

Because of the importance of age and education as basic dimensions of social structures, each of the eleven items in the index was analyzed by these two variables, using Goodman's procedure for multivariate contingency table testing (Davis, 1974). The results for the combined DAS-68 and DAS-71 samples, using data from black interviewers only, are presented in Table 17. Signs of the general age-education interaction reported above for the total index appear in a number of the items (1, 4, 5, 7, 8, 11), but, except for item 11, in none of these cases taken separately is significance reached. Apparently the age-education interaction is built up for the index out of small increments, rather than being located strongly in one or two individual items. A review of trends for all eleven items reveals in addition a cross-cutting result: college-educated respondents under 36 years of age are most frequently at the "high" end on these questions, while older, better educated (high school and over) respondents are usually at the low end. Thus the effect of education on attitudes is again seen to be different for different age levels.

Table 17 also tests for significance the partial association between each item and age, with education controlled; and each item and education, with age controlled. (The test involves constructing a model which omits a

TABLE 17 (*Sheet 1 of Table 17*)

Individual Racial Items by Age and Education*

1. Progress

Percentage "No Change"

Age	Education 0-11	12	13+
21-35	44 (77)	37 (92)	44 (48)
36-49	27 (123)	27 (70)	39 (46)
50-69	20 (133)	27 (30)	19 (21)

Tested	x^2	d.f.	p
3-way interaction	2.85	4	.58
Age and Item	20.68	6	.002
Education and Item	4.41	6	.62

2. Keep Down

Percentage "Keep Down"

Age	Education 0-11	12	13+
21-35	38 (76)	37 (93)	36 (49)
36-49	38 (120)	21 (70)	23 (47)
50-69	22 (127)	26 (27)	5 (22)

Tested	x^2	d.f.	p
3-way interaction	6.58	4	.16
Age and Item	22.76	6	.001
Education and Item	12.18	6	.06

Footnotes are presented on Sheet 4 of this table.

TABLE 17 (*Sheet 2 of Table 17*)

3. Trust

Percentage "Trust None"

Age		Education		
		0-11	12	13+
	21-35	18 (77)	18 (95)	18 (49)
	36-49	14 (126)	14 (72)	4 (45)
	50-69	10 (133)	0 (30)	0 (22)

Tested	x^2	d.f.	p
3-way interaction	9.19	4	.056
Age and Item	22.95	6	.001
Education and Item	12.68	6	.05

4. Clerks

Percentage "Less Politely"

Age		Education		
		0-11	12	13+
	21-35	49 (75)	39 (92)	47 (45)
	36-49	44 (121)	39 (69)	31 (45)
	50-69	20 (127)	31 (29)	27 (22)

Tested	x^2	d.f.	p
3-way interaction	5.42	4	.25
Age and Item	28.86	6	.000
Education and Item	6.14	6	.41

5. Jobs

Percentage "Many Places"

Age		Education		
		0-11	12	13+
	21-35	65 (77)	58 (94)	69 (49)
	36-49	63 (122)	61 (71)	64 (47)
	50-69	52 (124)	50 (30)	59 (22)

Tested	x^2	d.f.	p
3-way interaction	.56	4	.97
Age and Item	6.52	6	.37
Education and Item	2.47	6	.87

Footnotes are presented on Sheet 4 of this table.

TABLE 17 (*Sheet 3 of Table 17*)

6. Teachers

Percentage "More Interest"

Age	0-11	12	13+
		Education	
21-35	39 (71)	39 (89)	48 (46)
36-49	44 (114)	41 (61)	44 (45)
50-69	46 (121)	24 (29)	30 (20)

Tested	x^2	d.f.	p
3-way interaction	5.08	4	.27
Age and Item	5.55	6	.47
Education and Item	7.26	6	.30

7. Neighborhood

Percentage
"All Black" or "Mostly Black"

Age	0-11	12	13+
		Education	
21-35	18 (76)	13 (95)	19 (48)
36-49	14 (126)	11 (72)	4 (47)
50-69	15 (133)	10 (30)	9 (23)

Tested	x^2	d.f.	p
3-way interaction	3.20	4	.52
Age and Item	6.23	6	.40
Education and Item	6.56	6	.36

8. Best Means

Percentage "Violence"

Age	0-11	12	13+
		Education	
21-35	16 (75)	10 (90)	20 (47)
36-49	9 (125)	11 (72)	0 (45)
50-69	3 (133)	0 (30)	0 (23)

Tested	x^2	d.f.	p
3-way interaction	6.21	4	.18
Age and Item	27.28	6	.000
Education and Item	6.92	6	.33

Footnotes are presented on Sheet 4 of this table.

TABLE 17 (*Sheet 4 of Table 17*)

9. Second Means

Percentage "Yes, violence if. . ."

	Education				Tested	x^2	d.f.	p
	0-11	12	13+					
					3-way interaction	5.24	4	.26
21-35	33 (63)	37 (81)	26 (38)		Age and Item	6.54	6	.36
Age 36-49	35 (114)	39 (94)	14 (43)		Education and Item	12.5	6	.05
50-69	25 (129)	37 (30)	30 (23)					

10. Principals

Percentage "Black Principals"

	Education				Tested	x^2	d.f.	p
	0-11	12	13+					
					3-way interaction	7.62	4	.11
21-35	57 (76)	39 (93)	34 (47)		Age and Item	8.73	6	.19
Age 36-49	40 (124)	43 (70)	38 (47)		Education and Item	13.24	6	.04
50-69	49 (133)	27 (30)	48 (21)					

11. Fight for U.S.

Percentage "No"

	Education				Tested	x^2	d.f.	p
	0-11	12	13+					
21-35	26 (74)	12 (91)	33 (48)		3-way interaction	13.00	4	.01
Age 36-49	10 (120)	13 (70)	5 (43)					
50-69	7 (132)	17 (30)	9 (23)					

*Item numbering and titling follows that in Table 1; see Table 1 for complete wording. Items were dichotomized for the present analysis, as indicated by the heading shown above each sub-table here. Numbers of cases are shown in parentheses. Likelihood-ratio chi square statistics are presented. The combined DAS-68 and DAS-71 samples for black interviewers only are used. Read percentages as follows: for item 1, 44 percent of those 21 to 35 with 0 to 11 years of education responded "no change," the base being 77.

given partial association, and the chi square shown represents the level of significance at which that model can be rejected. Using the .05 level as our criterion, rejection of the model implies, in practical terms, that the partial association differs from zero.) Items 1, 2, 3, 4, and 8 all exhibit highly significant associations between age and the item: younger people show more skepticism of American progress toward racial equality, more distrust of white intentions toward blacks, and greater willingness to consider violence as needed to gain equal rights. Several other items show nonsignificant trends in similar directions (beliefs in job discrimination, desire to live in a black neighborhood, and to an extent, the item on willingness to fight for the United States in a major war). Only the items on black teachers (6) and black principals (10) and the follow-up question on use of violence fail to show an age trend.

We can therefore conclude that *most* questions dealing with militancy-black consciousness-alienation themes show the basic age trends indicated earlier for the index. At the same time, it is necessary to recognize that some of the items we had originally classified as dealing with these same themes do not show age effects or even age trends. We have no full explanation for these mixed findings, but two points are of interest. First, each of the three items that are *least* age-related reveals (albeit, after the fact) a possible defect:

a) The "teachers" item (6) deals with whether black or white *teachers* are more interested in black children, whereas we suspect that the more important point to respondents is whether black or while *children* receive different treatment. A similar situation is reported by Campbell and Schuman (1968) about policemen, for the difference most respondents feel strongly about is not that between black and white policemen, but rather between police treatment of black and of white citizens.

b) The follow-up item on use of violence (9) excludes those parts of the sample that had already chosen violence on the initial item.

c) The Principal item (10) as discussed earlier, is a somewhat slanted question in wording and format.

But even these exceptions, whatever the merit of our ad hoc explanations, serve to illustrate an important finding, namely, that age is not an all-powerful variable in black attitudes. Although age is clearly the strongest single background factor in black racial attitudes, not every item shows such a relationship and some that show it do so only weakly.

Moreover, it may be that even positive associations to age occur for different reasons on different items. The strongest and most consistent association with age occurs for the progress item (1). It is probable that this relationship reflects life experience in a simple and direct sense: older blacks grew up in a period when open segregation and not very covert discrimination were accepted parts of American life, and then lived through a decade or more when major symbols of inequality were challenged successfully both by white institutions and by black leadership. Having witnessed these changes in their own lifetimes, blacks now in their forties and older have indeed seen "much change." For blacks in their twenties, however, the changes that occurred during the fifties and early sixties were already over and part of history, and *their* perceptions were of riots and white police, of the continued minority status of blacks, and of the lack of much visible forward movement. If this interpretation is correct, then the sharp relation of age to the progress item is transitory and should disappear over time unless there are indeed further visible changes.

The other items showing correlation with age may represent a separate dynamic, though one difficult to distinguish operationally from the progress item at this point in time. Suspicion of whites and willingness to consider violence are both ideological beliefs different from the perception of progress, though no doubt linked to it causally at present. Since they reflect other forces that may continue to create an association with age—for example, the proclivity of youth for more aggressive action in the face of racial frustration—their correlation with age may persist in the future.

We have not thus far dealt separately with the item effects of education, except as it interacts with age. Although there are several borderline significance levels involving education and individual items, none is highly significant and we are inclined to regard them as too uncertain in reliability and meaning to warrant extended interpretation. The one trend here that seems most interesting—the fact that distrust of white intentions in items 2 and 3 is greatest among less educated older respondents—is not replicated in the Kerner-68 data. Our clearest interpretation of education is therefore that shown for the index as a whole: among older respondents education is largely unrelated to militancy, black consciousness, and alienation, while among younger (21-35) respondents the relationship is curvilinear, with the highest scores found among those with least education and most education, especially the latter.

Income

The measure of a respondent's income used in this analysis is reported total family income for the past year. Equating DAS-68 and DAS-71 is less simple here than for other background variables because of differences in question wording and also differences in real income due to inflation. Adjustment of the two years to the same scale and then additional adjustments to equate responses in terms of real income lead to an unusual and not quite mutually exclusive set of income categories. [8] However, the overlap is minor in terms of both dollars and cases, and despite the awkward nature of the final code categories shown in Table 18, it is likely that the effects of family income are reasonably well captured by this measure. Missing data, due mainly to unwillingness by respondents to report income, are large enough to require inclusion in the table.

There is no formal evidence of interaction among income, Year, and the Alienation Index ($F = 1.01$, d.f. $= 6$; 922), and Table 18 presents the combined DAS samples to provide an overall estimate of the relationship between income and the index. The association is small (1.3 percent explained variation) and just reaches significance ($F = 2.27$, d.f. $= 6$; 928, $p < .05$), hence it must be interpreted with considerable caution. [9] But there does seem to be an inverse relationship: higher scores are found among those with lower incomes. Despite the lack of significant interaction with Year, this negative association is clearest for the DAS-71 data, especially when only the black interviewer sample is used, as shown on the right side of the table. Since there is also little sign of any relationship in the Kerner-68 data (not presented), we infer that if the rather borderline results are indeed reliable, this must be due to an emerging trend—a trend present only obscurely in 1968 but appearing more clearly in the 1971 data.

We must admit to some uncertainty over whether any trend exists here at all—certainly it would be small in magnitude. If the relationship does prove reliable in future studies, it points to a conclusion long suggested by common sense but not recently discovered in fact: blacks most alienated from white society are those with lower incomes.

The departure from monotonicity at the low end of the income scale is even less certain in reliability than the overall trend, but it may reflect the apathy sometimes attributed to circumstances of life so depressed as to seem hopeless. It is also notable that the highest index scores of all for the total sample are associated with refusal to report one's income to the interviewer; it is tempting to speculate on motivational connections here, but we shall not pursue this line of inquiry.

The monotonic relationship between income and Alienation Index

---

[8]DAS-68 obtained family income on a monthly basis, while DAS-71 asked for family income for the previous calendar year. Even after change to the same annual basis, the categories are not quite the same. An adjustment upward of the DAS-68 income levels of 16 percent for inflation complicates the categories further.

[9]Neither adjusted means nor significance level are altered if education is included as an additional control.

TABLE 18

Alienation Index Scores by Total Family Income

Annual Family Income	DAS-68 and DAS-71 Combined Samples*		DAS-71 Black Interviewers Only**	
	N	Mean	N	Mean
Less than $4,000	171	4.00	38	4.82
$4,000 - $5,999	101	4.44	30	5.65
$5,568 - $7,999	206	4.26	27	5.32
$8,000 - $9,999	124	3.89	39	4.45
$9,744 - $14,999	160	3.74	40	4.37
$13,920 and more	128	3.88	29	3.91
(Missing data)	(52)	(4.51)	(11)	(4.86)

*Adjusted for sex, age, year, and race-of-interviewer.

**Adjusted for sex and age.

scores does not parallel the curvilinear one reported earlier for education. In the latter case, higher scores were associated with both high and low education. It is possible that education and income interact, as is implied by theories about the consequences of status inconsistency. It is certainly easy to hypothesize that, say, blacks with high education but low incomes would feel more alienated from white society. Our sample size does not allow this to be readily studied separately by race-of-interviewer, but for the combined DAS-68 and -71 samples (with Year, race-of-interviewer, age, and sex controlled) there are enough cases to allow a crude income-by-education variable. When this is done, however, the overall interaction component is not significant ($F = 1.16$, d.f. $= 8$; 867), and there are too few cases in strategic cells to provide grist even for much speculation. The results are shown in Table 19, along with the values (in parentheses) constructed from the additive model. None of the discrepancies is especially noteworthy, and it seems adequate for the present to recommend further pursuit of the findings for education and income taken separately, without need for more elaborate interpretation based on hypotheses of interaction.[10]

Occupation

Our previous results, together with some simple reasoning, suggest that the Alienation Index should show a curvilinear relationship to occupation, particularly among the young. The picture thus far is that black respondents *low* on the index tend to be neither high nor low in education, to be somewhat higher in income, and to be middle-aged or older. These findings suggest a picture of low scores as located in the middle range of socioeconomic status. The picture makes good sense, for it portrays the low scorer as someone who has done fairly well in social and economic terms in America, yet is not much influenced by the intellectual trends stirring black college students. In other words, this is the black counterpart of the white Middle-American, concerned mainly with his own family, home, and neighborhood, and fairly secure in income, status, and way of life.

In Detroit, the highly skilled male industrial worker fits this picture most clearly, for he has a relatively well-paying secure job at the top of the blue-collar status hierarchy. Our expectation was that these middle occu-

---

[10]A similar analysis was repeated on the Kerner-68 sample, with an N of 2,012. The increment in explained variation attributable to interaction is only 0.3 percent ($F = 0.8$, d.f. $= 8$; 1994), so that again we feel no need to call on non-additive models such as status inconsistency to explain variation in black racial attitudes.

TABLE 19

Mean Alienation Index Scores by Education and Income
For Combined DAS Samples*

	Completed Years of Education				
	0-8	9-11	12	13-15	16+
Less than $6,000	4.24 (4.33) [86]	4.23 (4.20) [90]	3.84 (3.97) [75]	4.57 (4.01) [19]	4.06 (4.99) [2]
$5,568-$9,998	4.46 (4.30) [73]	4.29 (4.17) [106]	3.80 (3.94) [109]	4.02 (3.99) [31]	4.16 (4.97) [10]
$10,000 or more	3.83 (3.92) [37]	3.55 (3.79) [58]	3.82 (3.56) [101]	3.37 (3.60) [50]	4.71 (4.58) [42]

*Underlined values are actual results obtained using a single Education-by-Income interaction variable as a predictor in MCA. Values within parentheses are effects based on an additive model where education and income are separate predictors. For both sets of values, means are adjusted for sex, age, Year, and race-of-interviewer. Bracketed numbers are N's on which interaction values are based.

pational level workers would be lower in Alienation scores than either white collar employees or lower status blue collar workers. And first analysis of the Alienation Index by occupation for men showed such a relationship: high scores at the two ends of the occupational distribution, low scores in the middle. For the combined DAS samples, men only, mean Alienation scores exhibit the following pattern:

		N
White collar	4.35	82
Foremen, craftsmen, and kindred workers	3.93	105
Blue collar	4.15	270

This fits exactly the expectation noted above.

However, the results just shown for the combined DAS samples fail to reach significance at the .05 level, and further analysis with controls (including education) of both that data set and the Kerner-68 data produces much inconsistency in results. In some cases the curvilinear trend disappears entirely, in others it persists but to a trivial degree. Thus for black interviewers, with age, Year, and education controlled, there is no association whatever ($E^2 = 0.1$ percent) between occupation and Alienation; even without the education control, the association is quite small (0.5 percent) and does not approach significance, though the expected trend is present to the eye. For the Kerner-68 full 15-city data, however, the association is small (0.4 percent) and decreases monotonically with higher occupational status. Reconciliation of these diverse trends would require a Ptolemaic set of assumptions about change over time and race-of-interviewer that are rather implausible, and impossible to confirm with these data.

We are inclined to treat the relationship of occupation to the Alienation Index as essentially zero, simply noting for future investigation the quite weak curvilinear trend exhibited above. We should also note that the curvilinear relationship between education and Alienation is maintained when occupation is included in multiple classification analyses, and that it is this U-shaped association that deserves more emphasis. Despite the obvious connections between education and occupational status, it seems to be education that is the more useful variable in understanding variation in Alienation scores.

Other Background Variables: Region of Socialization, Home Ownership, Marital Status, and Relation to Head of House

There are no signs of reliable relationships in the combined DAS samples between the Alienation Index and region of socialization, home ownership, or marital status. Or rather, borderline trends occur for bivariate associations (e.g., home owners have lower Alienation scores than renters, married lower than single, and Northern-reared lower than Southern-reared), but even such non-significant trends disappear virtually completely when controls are imposed for age, education, sex, Year, and race-of-interviewer. A detailed search for interactions has not been carried out, but at the level of multiple classification analysis none of the three variables appears to be an important independent source of variation in Alienation scores.

Throughout most of this volume we confine our sample and population definitions to persons who are heads of house or spouses of heads of house. For couples, families with one or both parents present, and households of unrelated individuals, this is an exhaustive definition, but for households including adult members other than head or spouse we do miss such persons as grown children, grandparents, and other relatives or non-relatives. However, the full Kerner-68 and DAS-71 data sets include such additional individuals, and we can draw on them to determine whether our delimitation leads to bias with respect to the total adult population. Comparing mean Alienation Index scores, there is no evidence in either study that the excluded adults are significantly different from heads and spouses. For the 15-city Kerner-68 sample, which is more useful in this case because of its size, we find that non-heads and non-spouses constitute eleven percent of the total sample (N=2830). However, the distinction between head and spouse on the one hand, and seven other categories of adults (e.g., grown siblings) on the other, accounts for only 0.4 percent of the variation in Alienation Index (abb.) scores (p < .10), and there is no obviously meaningful patterning to the average scores for the several categories. Thus, for the age range with which we deal (21-69), our results based on heads and spouses are very likely generalizable to all black adults in this urban population.

Conclusions

Our most important findings in this chapter are the relationships between Alienation scores on the one hand and age and education on the other. The main finding for age is consistent with all recent studies since the mid-sixties: younger blacks are considerably more alienated from white society than older blacks. (This may be a recent phenomenon, as Paige [1970] argues.) In magnitude this is the strongest background correlate of black racial attitudes, and its direction fits the basic facts of change reported in earlier chapters.

The finding for education is less strong and more complex and unexpected, but if replicated in future studies, it is of considerable importance. Alienation is highest among the least educated and the most educated respondents, though this curvilinear relationship appears only among younger persons.

The combined effects of age and education were presented in detail in Table 14. We repeat those basic results graphically here in Figure 4. The interaction between age and education is apparent in the U-shaped relationship among those 21 to 35, and in the differential decline in scores by age over the three educational categories. The figure sums up the primary findings from our data on basic background correlates of black alienation from white society.

Our analysis in this chapter did not demonstrate changes over time in

FIGURE 4

Mean Alienation Index Scores by Education and Age*

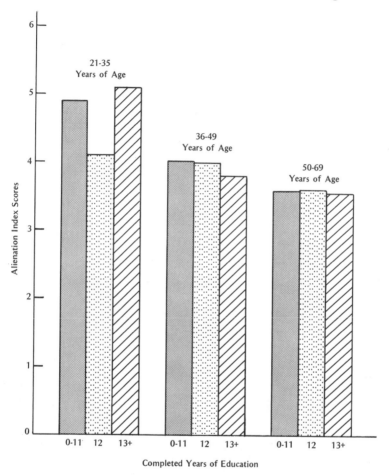

*Combined DAS-68 and DAS-71 samples. See Table 14 for detailed scores and base number of cases for each age-education category.

the background correlates of the Alienation Index. This is not surprising given the very short time period involved. It is hardly to be expected that demographic and socioeconomic correlates of black attitudes will change in a three-year period, or indeed that they should change markedly over even a much longer period. However, we did note two non-significant trends deserving further investigation. First, the strong sex difference in Alienation scores apparent in 1968 had declined in magnitude in 1971. Second, a negative association between family income and Alienation appeared in 1971, having been at most obscurely present in the 'earlier year. Both of these apparent changes are weak and uncertain in reliability, but they may presage trends of greater strength in the future. The discovery of a negative association with income would be of particular importance, but we must emphasize that the present finding, even if it turns out to be reliable, still leaves black alienation from white society remarkably *un*related to the dollars people have, or even (as shown in Table 19 above) to discrepancies between educational attainment and income. Indeed, the U-shaped association to education, along with other recent findings on black college students (Gurin and Epps, 1974), indicates that black alienation is not primarily a response to purely personal economic factors.

6

THE ALIENATION INDEX
AND OTHER ATTITUDES, BELIEFS,
AND ACTIONS

Our discussion to this point has focused on demographic and socio-economic correlates of the Alienation Index because these provide the most interpretable relationships in both a sociological and a causal sense. In this chapter we proceed in broader and more exploratory directions in an effort to understand better how the Alienation Index connects with a wide range of other attitudes, beliefs, and actions. Each of the three studies—DAS-68, DAS-71, and Kerner-68—offers useful variables for such an exploration. In no case do we have change data on the relationships, so we will be dealing separately with each study, drawing on its distinctive set of variables.

The two halves of the chapter differ in approach. The first half presents correlates of the Index from a largely inductive perspective, identifying those racial and non-racial variables most highly related to Alienation scores, as well as certain variables uncorrelated with them. Such an approach is often used in survey analysis, although rarely presented openly as such because of fear of accusations of "dust bowl empiricism." Used with caution—there are obvious problems of capitalizing on sampling error and of overly glib post factum interpretation—this approach can provide a better understanding of our central measure, aiding what is essentially an effort at construct validation. We avoid overlooking or obscuring important relationships simply because we had not thought to hypothesize them in advance. It is naturally hoped that the more important of these results will be replicated and pursued in later investigations.

The second half of the chapter approaches the data from a more theoretical standpoint. A series of problems are addressed—involving such variables as interracial contact, personal efficacy, economic, social, and specifically racial grievances, and self-reported participation in protest and other actions—and answers are drawn so far as possible from one or more of the three sets of data we have available. The chapter ends with attention to a perplexing finding which raises useful questions of substance, methodology, and meaning.

Part A: An Inductive Exploration

Other Racial Attitudes

Both the Kerner-68 and DAS-68 surveys contain a number of racial items in addition to those that compose the Alienation Index, and their association to the Index helps clarify its nature and implications. We concentrate our presentation on the more varied Kerner-68 survey, and since we are here not making comparisons over time for Detroit, it is useful to draw on the entire Kerner-68 fifteen-city sample of black respondents, ages 21 to 69—a total of 2,017 cases.[1] We will consider below the extent to which such an expansion of population definition geographically may affect results.

As might be expected, the Alienation Index (abb.) is related to practically all other black racial attitudes, and given the large size of the Kerner-68 sample, virtually all these associations are significant at well beyond the

---

[1]The sample consists of all heads and wives, ages 21-69, from fifteen cities: Baltimore, Boston, Brooklyn, Chicago, Cincinnati, Cleveland, Detroit, Gary, Milwaukee, Newark, Philadelphia, Pittsburgh, St. Louis, San Francisco, Washington. Analyses were also carried out including non-heads and wives; differences are slight, but will be noted below. Drawing on the total fifteen-city data (minus a 16-20 year-old age group that we have not dealt with in these chapters) allows us to increase greatly the size of the sample, and indeed generalize it, with little risk of altering results that would be obtained only for Detroit. For this analysis we have not weighted the Kerner-68 data, which means primarily that smaller cities are over-represented in the sample (Campbell, 1971); other analysis not presented here indicates that this makes little or no difference in findings where only attitude items are involved. The sampling exactness to be gained through weighting is small in substantive implication, and is offset by the increased problems in employing statistical inference and (more important) the distraction of attention from the logic of the analysis to moot points of sample definition differences.

.001 level. It would be redundant to report all such relationships, and therefore, for this purely empirical analysis, we focus on the strongest correlates of Alienation scores, although citing others as well where necessary or useful. Table 20 presents those items, out of fifty reviewed, which show an E^2 above 5.0 percent. The percentage of blacks asserting the position associated with *high* Alienation scores is also shown.

TABLE 20   (*Sheet 1 of Table 20*)

**Racial Beliefs and Attitudes Strongly Related
to the Alienation Index (Kerner-68)***

	Percent Taking Position***	F	d.f.	E^2
1. Believes almost all whites "dislike (Negroes)" (V. 128)**	14	149.7	(3, 1913)	19.0
2. A young (Negro) in America "doesn't have much chance [to get ahead] no matter how hard he works" (V. 95)	23	249.2	(1, 2029)	10.9
3. Believes it is "not possible for a white person and a (Negro) to be close friends" (V. 306)	6	166.6	(1, 2007)	7.7
4. If a riot broke out, would join it, rather than stay away or try to stop it (V. 291)	8	79.5	(2, 1971)	7.5
5. Favors discouraging white people from "taking part in civil rights organizations like CORE or NAACP" (V. 130)	8	134.2	(1, 1895)	6.6
6. Believes police in this neighborhood "rough up people unnecessarily" in the course of arrests (V. 61)	45	101.7	(1, 1509)	6.3
7. Agrees that "(Negroes) should not have anything to do with whites if they can help it" (V. 115)	8	64.4	(2, 2088)	5.8
8. Believes police in this neighborhood "do not show respect for people or. . .use insulting language" (V. 53)	46	87.6	(1, 1544)	5.4

Footnotes are presented on Sheet 2 of this table.

TABLE 20 (*Sheet 2 of Table 20*)

9. Rather own children have "only (Negro) friends" (V. 124)	4	54.2	(2, 1960)	5.2
10. Believes that own family income is lower than that of "the average white person with the same education" (V. 202)	32	50.9	(2, 1868)	5.2
11. Agrees that "there should be a separate black nation here" (V. 116)	5	56.3	(2, 2081)	5.1

---

*All associations in this table are significant beyond the .001 level.

**Project variable numbers from Kerner-68 are given for each item for technical reference.

***Percentage of respondents choosing alternative(s) presented in paraphrase of question. The number of alternatives is one more than the degrees of freedom shown first in parentheses.

Heading the list in Table 20 are two items that represent particularly well the term "Alienation from White Society." On the one hand, there is the belief in item 1 that most whites dislike blacks; the question is phrased in personal terms, and would seem to imply anticipation of negative interactions with individual whites. The four alternatives show a striking monotonic relation to Alienation scores:

> *"Do you think only a few white people . . . dislike (Negroes), many dislike (Negroes), or almost all white people dislike (Negroes)?"*

	N	Alienation means
Only a few	716	2.9
Many	931	4.3
Almost all	239	6.0
All (volunteered)	31	7.2

At the same time, high Alienation scores are also associated strongly with the belief (item 2) that the Horatio Alger ideal does not work for black Americans—that the system does not allow achievement by individual effort.

"If a young (Negro) works hard enough, do you think he or she can usually get ahead in this country in spite of prejudice and discrimination, or that he doesn't have much chance no matter how hard he works?"

	N	Alienation means
Can get ahead	1,559	3.6
Doesn't have much chance	472	5.5

Thus, *both* at the level of personal relationships and at the level of impersonal achievement in the status structure, those with high Alienation scores view white society in profoundly pessimistic terms. This devastating combination of beliefs about the consequences of being black in America would seem to justify fully the characterization "alienation from white society."[2]

The next set of items (3, 5, 7, 9, 11) highly related to the Alienation Index concern separation from whites in terms of personal friendship, participation in civil rights organizations, and even national identity. Such beliefs and preferences can be seen as flowing naturally from the conviction that most whites dislike blacks, though the actual dynamics would almost certainly be reciprocal. It should be noted that the percentage desiring such separation is very small, and with these items we are thus dealing with an extreme part of the black population both in proportion and in scores on the Alienation Index.

A quite different set of items in terms of content involve several types of police mistreatment (6, 8, and a third item on unnecessary police "frisking" that just misses the 5.0 percent criterion for entry into Table 20). These general belief items, it will be noted, divide the population much closer to the fifty-fifty line, and the finding here of their strong association to the Alienation Index is consistent with past research (e.g., Murphy and

---

[2]The mean correlation of each of these two items with the six items of the Alienation Index (abb.) is actually greater than the index interitem correlations. As reported earlier, the mean interitem correlation is .132; the mean correlation of the "dislike" item (number 1 in Table 20) with the six index items is .172, and the mean for the "get ahead" item (number 2) is .180. Thus these two items appear to be more central to the construct represented by the Index than are the individual index items themselves. (At the item level, the correlations between each of the two leading Table 20 items and the individual index items are uniform in size except for somewhat lower associations with the neighborhood preference item.)

Watson, 1970) pointing to police-citizen relations as a main source of tension in the black population. We will later look at actual experience with the police, as distinct from the general beliefs that appear in Table 20.

Finally, when we note that the Alienation Index relates strongly to intention to "join a riot" if one occurs, we recall that these data come from 1968, at the height of the urban rioting. Thus, the index predicts not only attitudes in the more abstract sense, but also an important "behavioral intention." Moreover, there is evidence that behavioral intention and actual behavior are by no means dissociated here, for the index is also significantly related (F = 23.0,d.f.= 2; 2100, p < .001) to reports of actual participation in a riot. The number of self-reported riot participants is quite small (N = 30), accounting in part for the low E^2 (1.1 percent), but the difference in index scale points (2.1) between participants and others is one of the largest for the entire set of Kerner-68 associations.[3] Moreover, the small number of self-reported participants is partly a function of the fact that serious riots had occurred by early 1968 in only six of the fifteen cities sampled, and thus behavioral intention was constrained by opportunity. (See Campbell and Schuman, 1968, pp. 53-55 for a discussion of the relation between intended participation and actual participation.)

It might seem from the skewness of the riot participation questions, as well as of those on separation from whites, that the Alienation Index is mainly useful for differentiating one small and extreme part of the black population. But the first question in Table 20, with which we began this discussion, cuts the sample at several different points, each step of which we saw to be related sharply to Alienation scores. Likewise, item 10 on black/white income comparisons divides the sample in a different way, yet shows a substantial relationship to the Index. Further, it should be emphasized that Table 20 omits a large number of highly significant correlates of the Alienation Index simply because their magnitude of association falls below the arbitrary level of 5.0 percent. For example, the following item divides the more "conservative" parts of the sample from most others, yet it is clearly related to the Alienation Index:

---

[3]This is the one question in the entire study where we have noted that omission from the Kerner-68 sample of persons not heads or spouses of heads of household has an apparent effect. Inclusion of such persons raises the number of self-reported riot participants to 41, the difference between means to 2.8, and E^2 to 2.4 percent. Since the same trends do not occur clearly on other militancy-type items, we are uncertain as to whether the present finding reflects something special about riot participation or is simply a result of sampling error.

"Some people say (the 1967 riots) are mainly a protest by (Negroes) against unfair conditions. Others say they are mainly a way of looting and things like that. Which of these seems more correct to you?" (V. 71)

	Percent	Alienation Means	
Mainly protest	65	4.4	$E^2 = 3.8\%$
Fifty-fifty (volunteered)	26	3.5	$F = 39.3$
Mainly looting	9	3.0	d.f. $= 2$; 1965
	100		$p < .001$

Thus the Alienation Index is nearly as successful in distinguishing the least militant parts of the population from the rest as it is in distinguishing the most militant.

As a final step in this inductive review, we may further connect the Alienation Index to other types of racial items of interest by reporting the strongest correlate of the index in each of the two DAS surveys. The DAS-68 survey included a number of racial items similar to those presented in Table 20, but our findings thus far would not be altered by their detailed review. One question, however, shows an exceptionally strong relationship to the Index and we note it here briefly:

"Some leaders want to organize (Negroes) into groups to protect themselves against any violence by whites. Do you think this is worthwhile or not?"

	N	Alienation Means	
Yes	181	5.3	$E^2 = 17.2\%$
No	397	3.4	$F = 119.8$
			d.f. $= .1$; 576
			$p < .001$

This item, like several we have considered earlier, focuses on white hostility towards blacks, and adds a counter-response by blacks. Thus it ties together in a single question the themes of perceived white oppression—here in the raw form of physical violence—and of black action, or rather reaction, against it. As such, it would seem to represent well the central features of the Alienation Index: the sense that whites and white society cannot be trusted to act fairly toward blacks and that blacks must defend themselves.

The DAS-71 survey introduced the replicated set of racial questions that we use in our index with a closed question on preferred racial self-designation that had not been asked explicitly in the 1968 surveys. The relation of that identity item to the Alienation Index provides a convincing ordering of the sense with which racial self-designation occurs:

"Here are some questions on racial issues. First, do you have a preference for one of these words: 'Black,' 'Negro,' 'Colored,' or 'Afro-American'?" (V. 174)

	N	Alienation Means	
Afro-American	21	6.1	
Black	144	5.1	$E^2 = 10.3\%$
Negro	89	4.0	$F = 10.8$
No preference (volunteered)	80	3.8	d.f. $= 4$; 374
Colored	45	3.6	$p < .001$

The aggregate change in terminology generally assumed to have occurred over the last years parallels neatly the aggregate rise in Alienation scores between 1968 and 1971 recorded in earlier chapters, and the two are linked here in the 1971 data at the level of individuals. This is probably a transient association, for as "black" wins out over past terms such as "Negro" and innovations such as "Afro-American," it should eventually lose its special ideological significance. For now, however, names count.

Non-Racial Attitudes (DAS-71)

DAS-71 was a replication of questions from eight earlier surveys, most of which were not racial in content (see Duncan, Schuman, and Duncan, 1973). Its virtue from our present standpoint is to allow examination of the relationship of the Alienation Index to a variety of questions in non-racial domains. Politics, family and sex roles, religion, and child-rearing are among the main areas covered in the 1971 survey. The questionnaire comprised approximately 125 closed questions, not counting racial items and background questions, and we reviewed 65 of these in relation to the Alienation Index, selecting the 65 both for broad coverage and for more intensive representation of areas likely to be correlated with the Index.

TABLE 21   (*Sheet 1 of Table 21*)

**Associations Between Alienation Index
and Individual Non-Racial Items (DAS-71)***

	Percent Taking Position**	F	d.f.	E^2
1. (Detroit) officials are doing a poor job (V. 135)	26	11.4	3, 368	8.5%
2. State officials are doing a poor job (V. 136)	23	10.9	3, 369	8.2%
3. Federal courts are doing a poor job (V. 68)	23	14.0	2, 337	7.7%
4. Denies "public officials really care about what people like me think" (V. 143)	60	9.6	3, 376	7.2%
5. Attends church infrequently or never (V. 198)	46	7.0	4, 378	6.9%
6. Dissatisfied with the protection of neighborhood provided by police (V. 142)	41	13.1	2, 374	6.5%
7. Believes Jewish people are less fair (than Protestants) in business dealings (V. 220)	50	9.1	2, 263	6.4%
8. Less interested in religion now than 10 or 15 years ago (V. 203)	26	5.0	2, 196	4.8%
9. Never asks God for help in making decisions (V. 207)	15	8.2	2, 375	4.2%
10. Would not object to changing national anthem from Star Spangled Banner to one easier to sing (V. 83)	71	14.4	1, 374	3.7%
11. Believes Jews are "trying to get too much power in the country" (V. 221)	35	5.7	2, 298	3.7%
12. Agrees that "public officials don't care about what people like me think" (V. 149)	64	4.6	3, 375	3.5%
13. Opposes idea that it is wiser for Protestants "as a general rule" to marry Protestants (V. 216)	50	5.3	2, 301	3.4%

Footnotes are presented on Sheet 2 of this table.

TABLE 21 (*Sheet 2 of Table 21*)

14. Does not consider divorce wrong (V. 215)	14	4.3	3, 377	3.3%
15. Does not consider gambling wrong (V. 214)	12	4.2	3, 378	3.2%
16. Most doctors are doing a poor job (V. 65)	10	5.8	2, 371	3.0%
17. Mistake to send American troops to Vietnam (V. 394)	82	10.7	1, 365	2.8%
18. Denies that "children born today have a wonderful future to look forward to" (V. 90)	27	4.8	2, 381	2.5%
19. Younger generation should be taught to think for themselves, rather than to do what elders think is right (V. 77)	58	8.6	1, 374	2.2%
20. Constitution needs frequent changes to bring it up to date (V. 82)	85	8.2	1, 374	2.1%

*All associations presented here are significant beyond the .01 level. The items have been stated or paraphrased in the direction associated with high Alienation Index scores, and are ordered in terms of magnitude of E^2. (Project variable numbers are included in parentheses.)

**Percentage of black respondents choosing alternative(s) presented in paraphrase of question.

Table 21 presents only those items which relate to the Alienation Index beyond the .01 level of significance.[4] Items are stated, usually in paraphrase, in the direction associated with high Alienation scores and, unless noted below, the association is monotonic. They are ordered according to the size of the correlation ratio (E^2), but small differences in explained sums of squares should not be stressed, since these values are not adjusted for degrees of freedom and they are of course subject to sampling error. For each question, the percentage of black respondents who asserted the paraphrased position is also shown.

Government officials. The most impressive set of associations in Table 21 occurs over a set of items evaluating public officials and institutions, with negative evaluations strongly associated with high Alienation scores (items 1,2,3,4). Apparently the construct "alienation from white society" is closely related to measures of "alienation from the political system." Other analyses of political change over time show black loss of confidence in government offices and officials to be substantial over the past several years (e.g., Miller, Brown, and Raine, 1973), and it seems likely that racial and non-racial attitudes for some blacks are indistinguishable in this sphere.[5] It is noteworthy that signs of such alienation in Table 21 are not

---

[4]The following methodological points should be noted: (a) DAS-71 was not limited to heads of house and spouses, and we have included in this chapter the full black subsample, ages 21-69, in order to maximize cases. The number of cases for this analysis is 384, reduced by inapplicable cases and missing data for individual items. See the last section in Chapter 5 for evidence that this sample enlargement is justified. It is quite unlikely that non-heads and non-spouses differ from heads and spouses, and even less likely that the small number of them (42) added here would change any conclusions. (b) Race-of-interviewer has not been regularly controlled in this broad item analysis, because of the smaller sample sizes for the separate DAS data sets, the expense of running so many multiple classification analyses, and the likelihood on the basis of previous findings that any interviewer bias would influence in the same direction most if not all of the attitude items involved. As a check on the latter assumptions, five items in Table 21 (1, 5, 10, 15, and 20) were repeated for black interviewers only; in no case was there a change in direction of association, and the resulting E^2's (9.3, 6.7, 1.1, 3.8, 0.6, respectively) are similar in magnitude to those reported in Table 21. Furthermore, since we treat each survey separately in this chapter, the problem encountered elsewhere of varying proportions of black and white interviewers does not arise. (c) Simple analysis of variance is employed here and in subsequent sections as the initial statistical tool, but as we will note at a number of points, assumptions of causal direction can seldom be made with certainty.

[5]However, studies of declining black trust in the political system may have overstated the degree of decline, for they generally compare current surveys using black interviewers with baseline surveys using white interviewers. As we saw earlier (Chapter 4), non-racial political items seem to be sensitive to race-of-interviewer effects.

restricted to any one level of government, but cover local, state, and federal officials, as well as "public officials" generally. Indeed, included are even the "federal courts," usually identified during the 1950's and 1960's as the bastion of civil rights, though we cannot be sure how many respondents paid attention to the adjective "federal" as distinct from other types of courts.

Religion. The next largest set of correlates is quite different in character, consisting of questions on religious involvement (items 5, 8, 9). Those high on the Alienation Index are less likely to report church attendance or dependence on God, and more likely to report decreased interest in religion over time. Gary Marx (1967), following Karl Marx, raised the issue of whether religion serves as an "opiate or inspiration" of the black masses. Marx found his measure of conventional militancy to be negatively related to indicators of religiosity. Our data clearly support Marx's finding, using our substantially different measure of Alienation from White Society. (Our Alienation Index is closer to what Marx calls "anti-white" attitudes.) Moreover, if we accept at face value respondent reports that they have personally experienced a decline in religious interest, we have the suggestion that religious and racial disenchantment have been growing together over the past decade, perhaps both replaced by a more activist political orientation.

Jews and Other Outgroups. Marx (1967) also deals with the question of whether black distrust of Jews is simply a reflection of distrust of whites generally, or has a distinctive source and cast. He provides evidence that blacks are not more anti-Semitic than whites, and that, while anti-Jewish stereotypes are held by many blacks, most blacks do not sharply distinguish Jews from whites generally and those who do are more apt to regard Jews favorably. Table 21 does not address these questions, but simply shows that high Alienation from White Society tends to be associated with negative beliefs about Jews. This is consistent with Marx's finding that "anti-white" attitudes—though not "conventional militancy"—are associated with his measure of anti-Semitism.

However, we can also address Marx's more general question on black-white differences in anti-Semitism, for we have white as well as black responses in DAS-71. On the item about whether Jews are trying to get too much power (number 11), 35 percent of the black sample answer in the affirmative, as against 15 percent of the white sample ($X^2 = 57.5$; d.f. $= 2$; p $<$ .001), a relationship that remains quite reliable even when education is controlled ($X^2 = 48.8$; d.f. $= 8$; p $<$ .001). The item on fairness by Jews in business dealings (number 7) yields more complex results, with black respondents more likely than white respondents to say *both* "more fair" and "less fair," as against "as fair"; the overall X^2 is significant, as are the partitions "more" vs. "as" ($\chi^2 = 32.4$; d.f. $= 1$; p$<$ .001) and "less" vs. "as" ($\chi^2 = 41.2$; d.f. $= 1$; p$<$ .001). We have not pursued this analysis to uncover all the bases of the non-monotonic relationship,but we find that the Alienation Index, our primary focus, shows a threshold-type relation to the item: Alienation means for "more fair" and "as fair" are almost identical (3.88 and 3.82, respectively) and both are significantly lower than the Alienation means for "less fair" (4.92). Thus higher Alienation scores seem likely to promote an increase in the percentage of blacks who believe Jews to be "less fair" in business dealings.

Whether high Alienation scores are part of a still more generalized ethnocentric stance is less clear. An item on whether Catholics are trying to gain too much power shows a positive association to the Alienation Index similar to that for the parallel items on Jews, though the relationship is less reliable (0.1$<$ p $<$ .05) and is therefore not included in Table 20.[6] Furthermore, DAS-71 asked blacks a direct question about racial intermarriage,[7] and the small group (N $= 29$) strongly opposed to such intermarriage has significantly higher Alienation scores (p $<$ .01) than those accepting it. On the other hand, item 13 in Table 21 shows that approval of mixed Protestant-Catholic marriage is *positively* related to the Alienation Index. This suggests a desire to decrease at least one kind of social barrier, though perhaps one that is of less meaning to respondents as their religious commitment declines. In summary, persons high on the Alienation Index tend to hold negative beliefs about Jews and Catholics and are opposed to racial intermarriage, but they tend to support religious intermarriage. These several findings can be reconciled if we picture high scorers as persons who emphasize racial division as the primary schism in society, and who stress unity within black ranks, at least so far as religion goes. This delineation fits the classic picture of ingroup solidarity in the face of perceived ingroup-outgroup division and outgroup hostility (Levine and Campbell, 1972).

Conventional Norms. Turning to a different type of item in Table 21, the relationship of Alienation scores to approval of gambling and divorce can be interpreted as representing a rejection of traditional middle class norms. Since we saw in Chapter 5 that the Alienation Index is not class-related in any simple or strong sense, it is unlikely that the basis of the present relationship can be found in differences in objective social class positions. Whether the relationship is ideological in a conscious sense

---

[6]Both questions about Catholics were asked of black Protestants only.

[7]This item was omitted from Table 21, since the table includes non-racial questions only, and was omitted from our index because it was not asked prior to 1971.

(e.g., rejection of "white standards") or simply reflects the association between two parallel types of "liberation" is less clear.

Other Correlates; Subjective Social Class. Finally, high Alienation scorers in Table 21 are more critical of doctors; more pessimistic about the future; more opposed to the Vietnam War; and more willing to encourage societal change in general ways. At a less reliable level ($.01 < p < .05$) and therefore not shown in Table 21, high scorers in DAS-71 also tend to show less trust in other people and their motives; to be more critical of the "Boy Scouts"; to support free speech for Communists; and to identify subjectively with the "lower class."

The last mentioned result on subjective social class is replicated in the Kerner-68 survey, where because of the larger sample size the finding is more reliable ($p < .001$) and can be more adequately analyzed. Alienation scores in that survey are distinctively high for the 8 percent of the sample claiming lower class identification, and are uniformly lower for the 6 percent upper, the 30 percent middle, and the 57 percent working class identifiers. This finding does not change when age, sex, and education are included in a multiple classification analysis, nor indeed vary when broad occupational breakdowns are introduced. These results suggest that explicitly "lower class" identification among blacks may represent a sense of personal exploitation in quasi-Marxist terms, although we have no direct evidence for this political interpretation of the social class measure.[8]

Summary. Overall, the various relationships we have described indicate a complex picture not easily conceptualized in conventional liberal-conservative terms. High scores combine rejection of tradition and an openness to change with a general criticalness and suspiciousness of all officials, institutions, and norms, especially those of a political nature. The label Alienation from White Society seems more than ever a fitting one, particularly if we understand White Society not only in the specific sense of black-white relations but in the broader sense of the institutions traditionally supported by and represented by white Middle-Americans.

As noted above with regard to items on Jews, we are able to look at white as well as black distributions on the non-racial items from DAS-71. Systematic presentation of such data would take us too far from our focus on the Alienation Index, but it is important to note that most of the items significantly related to the Index in Table 21 are also significantly related to race of respondent. However, the associations are such that if we con-

---

[8]Daniel (1972) seems to interpret lower class identification as due to a sense of purely personal economic and status disadvantage. This may be largely true, but does not account for its association with the Alienation Index—especially since the Index shows such a minimal connection to socioeconomic status.

TABLE 22 *(Sheet 1 of Table 22)*

**Black-White Differences on Four Items Associated
with the Alienation Index (DAS-71)***

1. *"Do you think (Detroit) officials and bureaus are doing a poor, fair, good, or very good job?"*

White	Black		Black Alienation Means
15%	26%	Poor	5.44
45	58	Fair	4.24
34	14	Good	3.44
6	2	Very Good	3.62
100	100		

N (1312)   (374)

$x^2 = 33.0$, d.f. $= 3$, p$<$.001

8. *"All things considered, do you think you are more interested, about as interested, or less interested in religion than you were ten or fifteen years ago?"*

White	Black		Black Alienation Means
33%	47%	More	4.1
39	27	Same	4.2
28	26	Less	5.2
100	100		

N   (669)   (199)

$x^2 = 14.5$, d.f. $= 2$, p$<$.001

Footnotes are presented on Sheet 2 of this table.

TABLE 22 (*Sheet 2 of Table 22*)

13. *"As a general rule, do you think it is wiser for Protestants to marry other Protestants or not?"*

White	Black		Black Alienation Means
58%	45%	Wiser	3.9
1	5	Unsure	4.6
41	50	Not Wiser	4.6
100	100		

N (1351)   (304)

$X^2 = 22.2$, d.f. $= 2$, p$<$.001

18. *"Do you agree or disagree with this statement: Children born today have a wonderful future to look forward to."*

White	Black		Black Alienation Means
46%	64%	Agree	4.2
11	8	Unsure	4.4
43	27	Disagree	5.0
100	100		

N (1344)   (384)

$X^2 = 41.1$, d.f. $= 2$, p$<$.001

---

*Numbering is keyed to Table 21 above.

---

ceive of the black population as moving over time in the direction of higher Alienation scores, then in some cases this movement will create a greater divergence in black and white attitude distributions, but in other cases it will create greater similarity. Table 22 presents two instances of each at a purely descriptive level, that is, without imposing controls for such differences as socioeconomic status. Thus, *all other things constant*, if black alienation becomes greater, blacks and whites should differ increasingly on evaluation of Detroit (local) officials and on Protestant-Catholic inter-marriage, but become more alike in pessimism about the future and in disinterest in religion. High Alienation scores do not therefore invariably imply ideological separation between blacks and whites; on certain issues the effect, perhaps paradoxically, may be to lead the races toward more similar views.

Non-Relations. We have been concerned thus far with items significant-ly related to the Alienation Index. It is also necessary to take note of the 35 items—out of the 65 we examined from DAS-71—that failed to show even marginally significant associations with the Index. Several important social and psychological spheres that do *not* appear to be part of, or connected with, Alienation from White Society, as least at the simple bi-variate level, are:

> Decision-making balance between husbands and wives
> Knowledge of names or terms of office of one's Senators [9]
> Sex-role allocation for children
> Marital satisfaction [10]
> Ideal family size preferences
> Formal and informal organizational ties
> Evaluations of scientists, of television, and of colleges

Thus, broad as the Alienation Index seems to be in its implications, it is by no means correlated with all other important attitudes and values. It is particularly noteworthy that beliefs about sex roles, which have also evi-

---

[9] It seemed possible that these political information questions would show a relationship to the Alienation Index once we controlled for variables that affect such learning more directly. Therefore a multiple classification analysis was run with age, education, and sex as predictors in addition to a three-point information scale (knows names of both Senators, knows one Senator, does not know either Senator). Alienation scores constituted the dependent variable. The relationship of political knowledge to Alienation scores did not approach significance in this MCA and no clear trend in means is evident.

[10] In fact, one marital satisfaction item does show a borderline (.05) relationship to the Alienation Index. High scores accompany extreme disappointment *and* extreme enthusiasm reported by wives about "the love and affection" they receive from their husbands, as against more neutral responses. It is possible that high scorers are simply more outspoken about such issues than low scorers, but since this does not happen in other marital satisfaction items, "chance" seems a more likely explanation for this isolated relationship.

denced some change over the past few years (Duncan, Schuman, and Duncan, 1973, pp. 28-30), do not reveal a connection to the types of racial attitudes we have been examining in this monograph.[11]

Part B: Theoretical Problems

Contact with Whites

Studies of racial attitudes have long been concerned with the effects of interracial contact—mainly, though not exclusively, on majority attitudes (Allport, 1958; Williams, 1964). In the 1968 DAS we explored racial contact from the black viewpoint, using the questions shown in Table 23.[12] The questions can be conceptualized into two types: those reporting degree of physical proximity (items 1 and 4) and those reporting the social content of the contact (items 2, 3, 5, and 6).

---

[11]The analysis reported in the text deals only with the full Alienation Index, but we repeated the same review of the 65 DAS-71 questions separately for four of the component items of the index: Keep Down (item 2 in Table 1), Jobs (5), Teachers (6), and Best Means (7). All four items tend to show similar relations to distrust of government officials, but they vary in the significance and degree of their relations to most of the other questions in Table 21, as well as to questions not shown in Table 21. We have not been able to discern any sub-patterns here, as would be the case if each of the four component Index items correlated with a distinctive and interpretable set of non-racial items from the DAS-71 data. On the contrary, there seems little thematic clarity to the set of correlates for each item. What does happen is that the Best Means and Keep Down items perform considerably better in the sense of having a greater number of significant correlates (20 and 15, respectively) than the Jobs and Teachers items (9 and 8). This result parallels similar findings of differential "richness" in correlational patterns noted at earlier points in our analysis, and we will return to this point in the concluding chapter. For now, we may note that this item level review failed to discover a sub-pattern of non-racial correlates of racial attitudes different from that produced by the Alienation Index as a whole.

[12]The DAS-68 data are unweighted in this presentation in order to simplify use of variance statistics. However, reanalysis using the income stratum weight for DAS-68 (Appendix A) reveals almost no change in the frequencies and means presented in Table 23. In particular, if the frequencies of contact are transformed into percentages, the weighted and unweighted figures differ in no case by more than 2 percent. Likewise, weighted and unweighted means are all within 0.2 of each other, and no conclusions about differences among means would be altered by use of weighting.

TABLE 23 (*Sheet 1 of Table 23*)

Alienation Index Scores by Contact with Whites (DAS-68)*

	N	Alienation Means	
1. *"In the two or three blocks right around here, how many of the families are white: none, only a few, many but less than half, or more than half?"* (V. 147)**			
None	78	4.0	
Only a few	363	3.9	$E^2 = 0.6\%$
Many but less than half	100	4.1	$F = 1.0$
More than half	49	4.4	d.f. $= 3, 589$
			$p =$ n.s.
2. (IF ANY WHITES) *"Do you and the white families that live around here visit in each other's homes, or do you see and talk to each other in the street, or do you hardly know each other?"* (V. 148)			
Visit homes	65	3.7	$E^2 = 2.0\%$
See and talk in street	189	3.7	$F = 5.1$
Hardly know each other	258	4.2	d.f. $= 2, 509$
			$p < .01$
3. (ASK EVERYONE) *"Apart from your neighbors are there (other) white people, including people from work, that you get together with socially or in recreational activities?"* (V. 149)			
Yes	222	3.6	$E^2 = 2.2\%$
No	375	4.2	$F = 13.1$
			d.f. $= 1, 595$
			$p < .001$
4. (IF WORKING)*** *"On your job do you work with only (Negroes) only whites, or with both (Negroes) and whites?"* (V. 102)			
Only Negroes	38	3.9	$E^2 = 0.0\%$
Only whites	15	4.2	$F = 0.2$
Both	363	4.0	d.f. $= 2, 395$
			$p =$ n.s.

Footnotes are presented on Sheet 2 of this table.

TABLE 23 (*Sheet 2 of Table 23*)

5. (IF WORKING WITH WHITES)***
   *"How often do you get together for
   lunch with whites you work with:
   often, sometimes, rarely, or never?"*
   (*V. 103*)

Often	260	3.7	$E^2 = 6.0\%$
Sometimes	57	4.7	$F = 7.9$
Rarely	24	5.0	d.f. $= 3, 372$
Never	35	4.8	$p < .001$

6. (a) (IF WORKING)*** *"Is your own
   immediate supervisor white or
   (Negro)?"*
   (b) IF WHITE) *"Do you feel he treats
   the whites and (Negroes) under him in
   the same way on the job?"* (*V. 251 and
   V. 252 combined*)

White supervisor, Equal treatment	251	3.8	$E^2 = 3.9\%$
White supervisor, Unequal treatment	56	5.0	$F = 8.1$
Black supervisor	91	4.2	d.f. $= 2, 395$
			$p < .001$

---

*DAS-68 data are here unweighted, but weighting by income stratum does not alter proportions of contact by more than 2% or Alienation means by more than 0.2 points.
**Original DAS-68 variable numbers.
***Retired persons were asked about last main job.

Close physical proximity as such has no apparent relation to overall Alienation scores. Whether in terms of residence (item 1) or at work (item 4), there is no evidence in Table 23 that mere physical presence influences or is influenced by the black racial attitudes we have been studying. [13] However, when respondents are divided by total family income (less than $8,000, $8,000 or more), among low income blacks those in mixed neighborhoods have *higher* Alienation scores than those in largely or entirely black neighborhoods (p < .05); for high income respondents, Alienation scores do not differ at all by degree of neighborhood mixture. Thus, if anything, neighborhood racial mixture as such seems to promote alienation from whites among lower income blacks. This finding is consistent with results from a recent more controlled study by Ford (1973).

When we turn to the social content of contact we do find more expected and reliable relationships, even though causal direction cannot be resolved in this cross-sectional analysis. Alienation scores are higher among those in mixed neighborhoods who do *not* know their neighbors at all (item 2 in Table 23); among those in mixed work situations who seldom or never eat lunch with whites (item 5); and among those who more generally lack social relationships with whites (item 3). Obviously, the lack of such primary relationships could be a cause of feelings of alienation toward white society, or the alienated feelings could lead to avoidance of interracial contact, or both may well occur. It seems most sensible to hypothesize a spiraling process, one which could begin either with white rejection of blacks or with black feelings of rejection, a process which might then cumulate rather readily.

---

[13]At the level of the individual items that make up the Alienation Index, the question of *preference* for black or mixed neighborhoods is parallel to the question in Table 23 on *actual* neighborhood contact (no. 1). When the items are crosstabulated, there is a significant association (p < .01): those who report living in all-black neighborhoods state a preference for such neighborhoods to a greater extent than do those in mixed neighborhoods. Unfortunately DAS-68 does not include a measure of neighborhood racial composition based on other than selfreport, but DAS-71 does include an assessment based on interviewer observation. For the latter study there is *no* apparent association between degree of neighborhood racial mixture and neighborhood preference. This inconsistency could be due to the change in time or to some other difference between the two studies, but it seems more likely that it results from the difference between objective and subjective descriptions of neighborhood racial composition. The DAS-68 association depends entirely on the difference between those who say "none" (no whites) and all other responses, the latter including "some" (whites). Since "some" can stand for very few or even one white, the difference between "none" and "some" may involve subjective preference or distortion more than actual fact.

The importance of the content of interracial contact is shown by the last question (6) on the race of the respondent's supervisor at work. Alienation means do not differ significantly by race of supervisor as such (the mean for all workers having white supervisors is 4.0, as against 4.2 for workers having black supervisors), but those reporting white supervisors divide sharply when we introduce the perceived treatment by the supervisor. Alienation means actually tend to be lower for those reporting non-discriminatory white supervisors than for those having black supervisors, and they are highest for those reporting discriminatory white supervisors. Again, we cannot be sure that it is the supervisor who "causes" the attitudes, rather than, say, the general attitude that causes the favorable or unfavorable perception of the supervisor. It does seem unlikely that the attitude influences selection of a job so as to have one race of supervisor or the other, although even this possibility cannot entirely be ruled out.

Personal Efficacy

The Kerner-68 survey included four items designed to measure "personal efficacy."[14] Concretely, the items contrast being able to plan ahead and act on one's plans, as against inability to plan because of chance or other unspecified factors that disrupt the best laid plans. As Table 24 shows, high Alienation (abb.) scores are quite significantly associated with the non-efficacious answer on each item. The reliability of the finding is not in doubt, but its meaning certainly is.[15] Are alienated respondents less efficacious in outlook, or are certain characteristics of respondents or of items misleading us?

----

[14]We are indebted to Gerald Gurin for advice in selecting the efficacy items, which are labeled "personal control" items in P. Gurin, *et al.* (1969). See this article for a discussion of distinctions among these and other "internal-external" items. See also Caplan (1970) and Forward and Williams (1970) for a discussion of these issues, with conclusions different from those reached here. Crane and Weisman (1972) provide results similar to ours but offer a rather different interpretation.

[15]Three of the Efficacy items were included also in DAS-68, and the results with the full index in this smaller sample tend to replicate those shown in Table 24. Only one of the separate items (item 3 in Table 24) reaches clear significance ($F = 7.8$, d.f. $= 2$; 587, $p < .001$), the other two showing smaller and non-significant trends in the same direction. It may be that further analysis would differentiate among the contents of these several Efficacy items—the one noted here speaks of how well one is able to carry out plans already formulated, as against those items that concern the desirability of planning as such—but the similarities in correlation in Table 24 do not encourage such additional differentiation.

TABLE 24

Alienation Index Scores by Personal Efficacy Items (Kerner-68)*

	Alienation Means	N	
1. *"Have you usually felt pretty sure your life would work out the way you want it to, or have there been times when you haven't been too sure of it?"* (V. 213)			
1. Pretty sure	3.6	738	$E^2 = 1.7\%$
2. Haven't been too sure	4.2	1353	
2. *"Do you think it's better to plan your life a good way ahead, or would you say life is too much a matter of luck to plan ahead very far?"* (V. 214)			
1. Plan ahead	3.8	1147	$E^2 = 1.3\%$
2. Too much luck to plan	4.3	936	
3. *"When you do make plans ahead, do you usually get to carry out things the way you expected, or do things usually come up to make you change your plans?"* (V. 215)			
1. Things work out as expected	3.6	833	$E^2 = 1.6\%$
2. Have to change plans	4.3	1216	
4. *"Some people feel they can run their lives pretty much the way they want to; others feel the problems of life are sometimes too big for them. Which one are you most like?"* (V. 216)			
1. Can run own life	3.9	1320	$E^2 = 0.6\%$
2. Problems of life too big	4.3	748	

*For items 1-3, the F ratio exceeds 28.0 in each case; for item 4, F = 13.1. Given 1 and 2,050 + d.f. for each item, $p < .001$ in all four instances.

To aid in interpretation, the four items were combined into a simple additive Efficacy Index and used as a predictor in a multiple classification analysis, with age, education, and sex included as control predictors. The five-point Efficacy Index initially explains 3.0 percent of Alienation Index variation (E^2), and this is decreased only slightly to 2.8 percent when the three controls are taken into account. The relationship remains a perfect monotonic negative one. Thus the differences in efficacy are not a function of demographic differences.[16]

It seemed possible that the obstacle of "luck" might be linked in the minds of some respondents to the white-controlled "system," and therefore the individual-system item presented earlier in Table 20 (item 2) was introduced as an additional control in a second multiple classification analysis. The Efficacy Index accounts for 1.4 percent of explained variation in Alienation scores above and beyond all these controls. The shrinkage is noticeable, but the net relationship nevertheless remains significant ($F = 8.2$, d.f. $= 4$; 2023; $p < .001$). Moreover, it is not at all clear that control on the individual-system item is appropriate, for other evidence suggests that the efficacy items are *not* generally interpreted in racial or political terms. We have random probe data on each of the four items in Table 24, and the free response explanations available fit well the face meaning of the items. "Efficacious" responses are typically explained in such terms as:

> "I have usually worked hard at what I wanted and I usually got it." (to item 1)
> "If you plan ahead, you have something to live for." (to item 2)
> "I don't depend on advice from anyone. Think it over, then act. Nothing else." (to item 4)

And the "non-efficacious" answers do indeed seem to deal with luck, fate, or real setbacks:

> "Sometimes everything seems to go wrong." (to item 1)
> "Things come up that you have no control about it." (to item 2)
> "Everything lies in the hands of fate. I can only try to makes things work." (to item 4)

---

[16]The relationship holds with equal strength *within* the age category 21-35, with education and sex controlled. The Efficacy Index was also run separately for the whole sample against each of the six items that compose the Alienation Index (abb.). With the exception of the Neighborhood item, all show the same negative monotonic relationship to Efficacy—which provides some assurance of the homogeneity of the Alienation Index in relation to this quite separate personality measure. On the looser connection of the Neighborhood item to the rest of the Alienation Index in 1968, see Chapter 3, footnote 3, above.

FIGURE 5

Efficacy Index Scores by Alienation Index (Kerner-68)

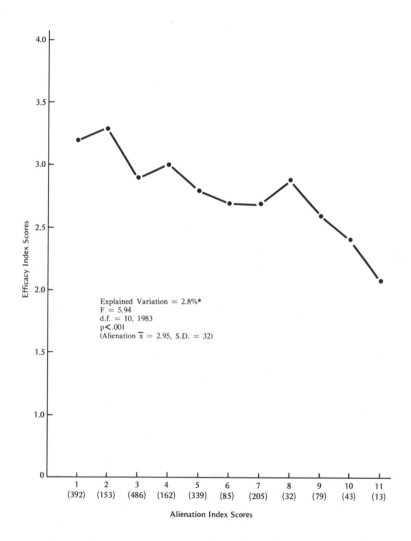

Explained Variation = 2.8%*
F = 5.94
d.f. = 10, 1983
p<.001
(Alienation x̄ = 2.95, S.D. = 32)

*Beyond that accounted for by sex, age (21-35, 36-49, 50 + years), and education (completed years 0-8, 9-11, 12, 13-15, 16 +). The F ratio and d.f. are also calculated on this increment. Without controls, the Alienation Index accounts for 3.6 percent of the variation in Efficacy Scores.

Despite the fact that the four efficacy items came at the end of a largely racial questionnaire, only one of the 169 random probe explanations mentions race explicitly, and it does so in the context of an efficacious response:

> "Plans and goals give incentive. The hardships of being black can be softened if the future is looked to as a challenge." (V. 214)

Thus it does appear that the relationship of the Alienation Index to this measure of efficacy is not the result of some simple artifact or contamination of indices. At the level of face validity, Alienation from White Society appears related to a larger pessimistic view of the forces opposing individual effort. Somewhat contrary to Gurin, *et al.* (1969), one might speculate that while impersonal chance or fate and racial discrimination are obviously quite different in nature, the personal tendency to emphasize external as against internal obstacles to success or happiness in life may carry over to both. As so often in this chapter, however, we must caution against oversimplified causal assumptions, adding in this case a reminder that the Alienation-Efficacy association is not an unusually strong one. But certainly it would seem to deserve further research. Figure 5 summarizes graphically the basic Alienation-Efficacy relationship, this time treating the Alienation Index as an independent variable so that we can see the shape of the association (controlled for age, sex, and education) over the entire index range. Despite some irregularities, probably due to index points based on small numbers of cases, the relationship is approximately monotonic over the entire eleven-point scale. The slope is sharpest and least ambiguous at the two ends of the scale, which means that low as well as high Alienation scores are distinctive in Efficacy level.

Personal Grievances

The Alienation Index includes questions on black beliefs about discriminatory actions of whites, for example, of white clerks and white employers. None of these questions, however, call for direct reports of actual personal experiences, nor did any of the racial items discussed in Part A of this chapter. We now present results showing smaller but still reliable associations between the index and several types of specific personal mistreatment reported by respondents. Table 25 lists five such items from the Kerner-68 survey, two on abuse by police, one on overcharging by stores, and two on job discrimination. In each case, those who report a personal grievance have higher Alienation scores than those who do not. One other police-abuse question on unnecessary frisking shows a similar but small and non-significant trend. Thus, in general, personal grievances do appear to be related to Alienation (abb.) scores, though perhaps a bit less so with regard to police abuse than for the employment area.[17] However, personal experiences with discrimination do not seem to be as important a factor in promoting high Alienation scores—assuming that is the causal direction— as are general beliefs about discrimination. This is not surprising, for attitudes are generally more highly correlated with other attitudes and beliefs than with any background, behavioral, or experiential factors.

TABLE 25

Relationship of Personal Grievances and Alienation Index (Kerner-68)*

	Percent Taking Position	E^2
1. Reports having experienced personal insult or disrespect from police (V. 54)	20	1.2%
2. Reports having experienced rough physical abuse by police (V. 62)	6	0.6%
3. Reports being unfairly overcharged often in neighborhood stores (V. 255)	28	4.5%
4. Reports having experienced discrimination in hiring (V. 82)	35	3.4%
5. Reports having experienced discrimination in terms of job promotion (V. 84)	17	2.5%

*Questions are paraphrased in the direction associated with high Alienation Index scores, and percentage giving paraphrased grievance is shown. All relationships are significant at the .01 level of confidence, and all but item 2 at well beyond the .001 level.

---

[17]The difference in Alienation means between the police and the employment items might at first thought be attributed to the inclusion within the Alienation Index of an item on beliefs about job discrimination. However, the abbreviated Index used for Table 25 does not include this item. Nor do the differences between the police and employment items seem explicable in terms of the number of, or distribution of, cases over the categories of the several variables.

It may be noted that *none* of the above personal grievance items specifies the race of the person(s) responsible for the unfair treatment, and the police items do not even specifically attribute abuse to racial factors. We did find in answer to another question about the difference between black and white policemen that greater trust in black policemen is significantly associated with high Alienation Index scores; yet it is also clear that most blacks (over 80 percent) regard the race of the policeman as irrelevant to the treatment, good or ill, he provides black citizens. We are safest to regard the correlation between grievances and Alienation scores as centering on, but probably more general than, racial grievance as such.

The DAS-68 survey also included several questions on police and employment which replicate closely the results presented in Table 25 and need not be repeated here. In the employment area, there is an added question on whether the respondent has experienced discrimination *more* than once, and again those saying yes have significantly higher Alienation scores ($F = 8.9$, d.f. $= 1$; 159, $p <$ .01) than those who report only one incident. DAS-68 also included a more general open question on grievances:

> *"Thinking back, what was the worst experience you have ever had with whites or with a white person?"* (V.243)

	N	Alienation Means	
(Code highest number)			
1. Denies any bad experience	257	3.7	$E^2 = 2.2\%$
2. Mentions act of discrimination	100	4.2	$F = 3.8$
3. Mentions verbal abuse	98	4.0	d.f. $= 3$; 522
4. Mentions physical abuse	71	4.5	$p <$ .01

Approximately half the sample did not report any bad experience with whites in reply to this rather leading question, while at the other extreme, 14 percent reported physical injury of some type. Those reporting no bad experience have the lowest Alienation scores, while those reporting the most serious injury have the highest scores. The ordering of the two middle categories, "discrimination" and "verbal abuse," is debatable, hence the apparent reversal of means does not indicate inconsistency. What is clear is that reports of negative experiences with whites are consistently associated with higher Alienation scores, though the quite plausible causal sequence in which negative experience causes alienated attitudes cannot be demonstrated with these data, and it is not impossible to conceive of a reciprocal process. Overall, on general and specific questions alike, reports of personal grievances and Alienation scores are directly correlated.

Subjective Economic Condition

The Kerner-68 survey included several questions involving self-assessment of one's own economic status. Table 26 shows that the dissatisfaction of respondents with their financial situation is significantly associated with higher Alienation (abb.) scores for the total sample. When the sample is broken by family income, the percentage of persons who are dissatisfied declines with each step upward in income, but nevertheless, within income categories an association between dissatisfaction and Alienation scores prevails at each level. For example, 42 percent of those with an income less than $4,000 are "not satisfied at all," as against only 12 percent with an income of $10,000 or more; yet the Alienation means for these two dissatisfied groups are almost identical. Thus a rise in income decreases dissatisfaction in this sphere, but those who *are* dissatisfied continue to manifest relatively high degrees of alienation from white society.[18]

Within the total sample or any of the income categories, the main jump comes for those "not satisifed at all," there being little difference between the "pretty well" and "more or less" satisfied. This may be simply a result of the rather mild difference in wording between the latter two levels, but more consistent with the maintenance of the association at all income levels is the hypothesis that the propensity to feel "dissatisfied" with one's income is linked directly to the tendency to express alienated sentiments on a variety of other non-economic items. As to why these joint tendencies continue to hold even at higher income levels, one can invoke either a personality model (e.g., picturing generally disgruntled individuals) or an expectation model (cf. Crawford and Naditch, 1970). The expectation model would turn on the fact that even incomes of well above $10,000 in 1967 could easily be exceeded by high expectations based on education, comparisons with similar whites, or some other reference point. It does not follow, however, that black income expectations rise inevitable at the same rate as black incomes, for as we noted above, Table 26 shows clearly that the proportion of dissatisfied persons goes down as income increases.

Opposed to an expectation model, at least a simple economic one, was our failure in Chapter 5 to find interaction effects of education and income

---

[18]This implies some negative correlation between income and the Alienation Index; such exists, but as reported earlier (or can be calculated here) it is tiny and non-monotonic.

TABLE 26

Alienation Index Scores by Dissatisfaction with Income (Kerner-68)

"In general, would you say you are pretty well satisfied with your family's present financial situation, more-or-less satisfied, or not satisfied at all?" (V. 199)

	N	Alienation Means	
1. Pretty well satisfied	875	3.8	$E^2 = 1.9\%$
2. More or less satisfied	660	3.9	F=20.1
3. Not satisfied at all	565	4.6	d.f.=2, 2100
			p<.001

Within Income Categories*

	Under $4,000		$4,000 - $7,999	
	Percent	Alienation Means	Percent	Alienation Means
1. Pretty well satisfied	30	3.6	39	3.8
2. More or less satisfied	28	3.8	31	3.8
3. Not satisfied at all	42	4.7	31	4.4
	100 $E^2 = 4.3\%$		100 $E^2 = 1.5\%$	
N	(468)		(843)	

	$8,000 - $9,000		$10,000 and above	
	Percent	Alienation Means	Percent	Alienation Means
1. Pretty well satisfied	50	4.0	54	3.7
2. More or less satisfied	34	3.9	33	4.0
3. Not satisfied at all	16	4.6	12	4.8
	100 $E^2 = 1.1\%$		100 $E^2 = 2.1\%$	
N	(313)		(384)	

*Total 1967 family income reported by respondent and recoded here.

on Alienation scores. We also, in Kerner-68, asked respondents themselves to make a subjective controlled comparison of their family income with that of whites:

"I would like you to think of white people who have the the same education you have. As far as the present income of your family, do you think you are better off, worse off, or in about the same position as the average white person with the same education?" (V.202)

	N	Alienation Means	
1. Better off	281	4.0	$E^2 = 5.2\%$
2. About the same	981	3.5	$F = 50.9$
3. Worse off	609	4.8	d.f. = 2; 1871
			$p < .001$

The question seems a bit difficult to use in a general survey, and we cannot be certain that the controlled comparison was widely understood. The results do indicate, as expected, that those who see themselves as worse off than comparison whites have higher Alienation scores. However, the not insignificant number who see themselves as *better* off also have higher Alienation scores ("better" vs. "same," $F = 10.8$, d.f. = 1; 1262, $p < .001$). Perhaps mainly out of pride, though possibly in part due also to misunderstanding, respondents high on the Alienation Index tend to say they have done better financially than whites with the same education. Only three random probe responses are available for the response "better off" and they suggest that both these factors are operating:

"Because I have more money than the average person."

"White people are never satisfied with what they have and they are unhappy. We have to make do."

"I feel I am better off because I feel I live better than the white person with the same education as I have, even though he may get more money. We put ours to good use so we can live as we do."

Thus we suspect that the response "better off" reflects a mixture of black pride and respondent misunderstanding that is difficult to disentangle in these data.

The explanations of "worse off," on the other hand, show little ambiguity (e.g., "They can always get a better job than me"), and the same is true for the alternative "about the same" (e.g., "Most jobs require education today—I talk with white fellows with no more education than I have and they aren't any better off.") The elevation of Alienation scores for "worse off [than whites]" is consistent with an expectation model, but cannot prove it convincingly since the "worse off" response may simply reflect the same dissatisfaction and alienation already manifested in the other items, rather than registering a separate causal factor. However, if we use the comparison-with-whites item as a control, we find that the relationship in Table 26 between income dissatisfaction and Alienation tends to disappear. Such a control is not unambiguous in nature— for if the two income items are simply indicators of the same construct, it makes little sense to use one as a control for the other—but the result does suggest that the association between income dissatisfaction and Alienation has as a component a sense of financial deprivation relative to whites.

Attitude and Action

Any survey of attitudes and beliefs must be concerned with the extent to which these are related to actions outside the survey. We have no direct measures of such actions,[19] but we do have respondent reports of their own behavior in two areas: protest activity and political participation.

We have already noted (on p. 82) that self-reported riot participation is strongly related to the Alienation Index. What about forms of protest that do not involve violence? The Alienation Index in DAS-68 is related significantly (p < .001) to self-reported picketing "against a place that was unfair to Negroes," and to an index based on self-reported participation in boycotts, marches, sit-ins, and similar examples of non-violent direct action. Yet on a question from Kerner-68 about having "contributed money to any civil rights organizations" during the past five years, there is actually a small reverse relationship: those who say no have higher Alienation (abb.) scores than those who say yes (F = 4.2, d.f. = 1; 2107, p < .05). With age controlled the association is no longer significant, but it does not reverse in direction. (Unfortunately, the survey did not obtain information on the nature of the organizations to which contributions were made.)

Thus the Alienation Index seems clearly related to active protest, but not to a more passive and traditional expression of involvement for civil

---

[19]We do have some interviewer ratings of behaviors (e.g., cooperativeness) within each survey, which presumably carry over into other forms of interaction. Simple bivariate analysis does not reveal any associations between such ratings and the Alienation Index. Interviewers also estimated the respondent's skin color on a four-point scale from dark to light in both Kerner-68 and DAS-68. As Edwards (1973) and others have shown such estimates are related to socioeconomic status, but in the present analysis we find no evidence that respondent skin color is related to Alienation scores.

rights. With the latter finding in mind, it is not surprising that when we turn to conventional forms of political participation, there is no association to the Alienation Index. Only a single question (from DAS-71) is available: "Have you ever helped campaign for a party or candidate during an election—like putting in time or contributing money?" Those who answer yes to this question—31 percent of the black sample—tend to have lower Alienation scores, though the difference does not approach significance. A control for age in a multiple classification analysis eliminates this trend, apparently because older age is related to both greater participation and lower Alienation scores, but the trend is not reversed. In sum, the Alienation Index is positively related to a variety of forms of direct protest action, but it is unrelated or even slightly negatively related to more conventional participation in political competition. The latter finding accords with our earlier one that the Index is unrelated to knowledge of the names and terms of office of United States Senators.

Apparent Ambivalence

Throughout most of this volume we have treated the Alienation Index as a unidimensional bipolar scale, with unambiguous "high" and "low" ends. We are well aware that the index is not really so simple, and that the various items are heterogeneous in content, modestly intercorrelated, and can readily be conceived to comprise at least several potentially different dimensions. For much of our analysis the oversimplified single-factor assumption has worked reasonably well, but in several instances (for example, the item comparing own income to whites) non-monotonic relationships appeared. In this last section, we focus on one such intriguing hint of complexity.

Table 28 presents an important item on obeying the law which revealed an unexpected relationship with the Alienation Index. Predictably, those who believe that blacks have *less* duty than whites to uphold the law have higher than average Alienation scores. But the same is also true of those who believe blacks to have *more* than average duty to uphold the law. Both the paired contrasts ("more vs. same" and "less vs. same") are highly significant, even though the difference in Alienation means is somewhat smaller in the first contrast than in the second. The issue is: Why should high Alienation scores be associated with *both* upholding and disobeying the law? One can entertain some exciting substantive explanations, but before any can be admitted to serious consideration, more obvious methodological and analytic possibilities need to be pursued.

One possibility of considerable importance to our use of the Alienation

TABLE 27

Duty to Obey the Law and the Alienation Index (Kerner-68)

"Generally speaking, do you feel (Negroes) have more, less, or the same duty as whites to obey the law?" (V. 79)

	N	Alienation Mean
More	107	5.0
Same	1845	3.9
Less	114	5.5

	More vs. Same vs. Less	More vs. Same	Same vs. Less
E^2	3.2%	1.1%	2.5%
F	33.9	22.6	50.0
d.f.	2, 2063	1, 1950	1, 1957
p	$< .001$	$< .001$	$< .001$

Index is that the several items composing the index are related differently to the law question. Since relatively high (though not perfect) Index scores can be obtained in a variety of ways, some of these combinations could lead toward one association and some toward the other. For example, the "best means" question could be associated with breaking the law, while the "progress" question with upholding it. To investigate this possibility we cross-tabulated the law question with each separate item from the Alienation Index (abb.). Our finding is that *all* six items present much the same relationship to the law question as does the full index. Even for the "best means" question, of those who say blacks have more duty to uphold the law, 23 percent think violence may be necessary to win equal rights; of those who say blacks and whites have an equal duty before the law, only 13 percent are ready to advocate violence; and of those who say blacks have less duty to be law-abiding, 32 percent lean toward violence. Thus the relationship for the "best means" question is much like that for the other five questions. Heterogeneity within the Index does not account for the curvilinear relationship.

A second possibility is that the Alienation Index and some other variables interact in non-additive ways to create one kind of person who believes in going against the law and another even more exceptional person who believes in especially high standards of law-abidingness for blacks. The possible lines of analysis here, of course, are many, and we examined only several of the most obvious ones. Table 28 shows that the basic curvilinear pattern persists within categories of sex, age, education, and Efficacy scores. The pattern does shift in interpretable ways: upholding the law is emphasized more by women than by men, more by older than by younger persons, more by high school graduates than by those with less than high school (the reversal in the college category may well be due to small samples but may also reflect the curvilinear association of Alienation with education we reported in Chapter 5), and more by high Efficacy than by low Efficacy scorers. *Yet it is surprising that in no case does a monotonic pattern appear,* with Alienation scores highest for "less duty," middling for "same duty," and lowest for "more duty."

It is conceivable that the interaction sought is more complex than any shown in Table 28 (e.g., four-way) or that it involves other variables not considered there. But at this point we turned instead to the random probe responses available for the "law question" and found a more plausible solution to the problem. (For a discussion of the random probe procedure, see above p. 25). Those respondents who say "same duty as whites" give expected explanations (e.g., "The law is the law and everybody should obey it."), and the one explanation available for "less duty" also fits the closed response ("Because the laws were made to hinder us and help the white at the same time. It provided loopholes for the whites."). But consider the five probe responses available for the "more duty" closed alternative:

"Whites can get away with things Negroes can't. Police see a Negro doing the same thing as whites, but the Negro would get beat on the head and sent to jail for it."

"The Negroes have to be more careful because of the racial pressures."

"Because we're colored. Because white people make the law, break it, and do like they want."

"I do because they get picked up more at night. Also they can't walk downtown at night without being searched."

"Because to me that's the way it seems. They expect more from us. Even when you to to court, the judge expects more. You have to have more witnesses and be able to show concrete, sound evidence for everything."

TABLE 28

The Alienation Index - Law Question Relationship by Sex, Age, Education, and Efficacy (Kerner-68)

Duty of Blacks to Obey Law	Sex				Age					
	Men		Women		21 - 35		36 - 49		50 - 69	
	N	Alienation Mean	N	Alienation Mean	N	Alienation Mean	N	Alienation Mean	N	Alienation Mean
More than whites	55	4.6	52	5.4	52	5.1	32	4.9	23	4.8
Same as whites	746	3.9	1099	3.8	655	4.4	692	3.7	498	3.4
Less than whites	56	5.4	58	5.6	55	5.8	39	5.6	20	4.5

Duty of Blacks to Obey Law	Education						Efficacy Index					
	0 - 11		12		13 & Over		Low (1-2)		Med. (3)		High (4-5)	
	N	Alienation Mean	N	Alienation Mean	N	Alienation Mean	N	Alienation Mean	N	Alienation Mean	N	Alienation Mean
More than whites	62	4.9	30	5.3	5	4.7	43	5.4	28	4.3	31	5.2
Same as whites	1051	3.9	519	3.8	91	3.8	671	4.3	438	3.9	636	3.4
Less than whites	75	5.7	27	4.6	4	6.4	41	6.2	31	4.9	26	4.8

These explanations indicate that "more duty than whites" is not really heard as "duty" in the normative sense, but rather as "need" to obey the law. Respondents are saying that blacks have to be more careful to stick to the law than whites because blacks are more closely watched, more easily arrested, more readily convicted. (For evidence that this may well be true even with traffic violations, see Heussenstamm, 1971.) Once we realize that this is the interpretation given to "more duty," it is evident that high Alienation scores could sensibly be associated with that alternative. Moreover, the differences in Table 29 by sex, age, education, and Efficacy may reflect differences in caution as well as, or instead of, any special adherence to the law.

We have not, to be sure, explained why some high scorers interpret the question in one way and some in another way. But that is a less interesting problem and we shall not attempt to pursue it here. What is clear is that the Alienation Index is not at fault, an important interaction has not escaped our analysis, and the original "curvilinear" mystery about *duty* to obey the law has vanished.

Conclusions

The Alienation Index was constructed from a set of items selected originally to measure change in a number of facets or aspects of black consciousness, militancy, and alienation from whites and white society. The later creation of a single index was a practical convenience for purposes of further analysis, which received some justification from the (modest) positive correlations among the component items and the lack of obvious clustering into distinct subsets. Despite the somewhat heterogeneous appearance of the items, the first half of this chapter provides further evidence that the index as a whole does measure primarily feelings of alienation from white society. Its strongest correlates from our three surveys are other items which deal with expectations of open hostility from whites. Only slightly less strong is the sense that blacks cannot expect a fair chance within the society, either as persons working to achieve or as citizens dealing with societal representatives such as police or politicians. In fact, even when race is not mentioned explicitly, the index is associated with beliefs that the larger political system is unresponsive and untrustworthy. Thus, it is important to recognize that black alienation, as represented by high scores on this index, occurs at both the personal level of primary group relationships and at the level of citizen-to-society connections. It involves distrust of the possibilities of friendship across racial lines in daily life, and of the possibilities of fair treatment for blacks in the larger occupational, political, and other major structures of the total society.

The Alienation Index measures beliefs and attitudes, not behavior. We do not have direct observations of action, but where we have reports at a behavioral or quasi-behavioral level, they show some but not all of the expected associations with the index. High scorers on the index report fewer friendly relations and more negative experiences with individual whites and white societal representatives such as the police. However, the simple fact of living or working in a mixed as against a segregated setting reveals little or no relationship to index scores. It is friendship, not physical proximity, that seems to count, although we have no way of specifying causal direction. Considering actions taken by the respondent himself, high scorers are more likely to report having participated in a variety of protest activities, from boycotts to riots, but this association does not extend to more conventional forms of political involvement such as financial contributions to candidates or organizations.

When we turn to other attitudes or dispositions of a non-racial nature, we find an unexpected negative association between sense of personal efficacy and the Alienation Index, one which is maintained under a variety of controls. No definitive explanation for this can be tested with our data, but one hypothesis would follow lines of thought developed originally by Rotter (1966) regarding internal and external sources of control. Different as are white discrimination and "chance" or "fate," both are external forces which do occur in life, and the tendency to perceive and emphasize various such external barriers to achievement or happiness may be a quite general factor, as Rotter and others have maintained. This need not be taken to mean that the external forces are unreal, but only that persons vary in sensitivity to them. Similarly, discontent with one's income is related to high Alienation scores at medium as well as low income levels (though the *amount* of discontent decreases with increasing income), a finding that again carries broader personality implications.

Other apparently non-racial attitudes are also related to the Alienation Index, for example, rejection of traditional religious practices and involvement. Thus racial attitudes clearly extend into many spheres of life not racial in manifest content. However, it is not true that racial issues so pervade black consciousness that they are associated with all other social and political issues. We found little or no evidence that the Alienation Index correlates with attitudes toward sex roles, with husband-wife division of labor, with political information, or with a variety of other measures available for review. Our analysis of such possible correlates was not exhaustive, and it is always possible that certain interactions or suppressed correlations went unrecorded; but it seems clear that scores on the Alienation Index—or probably any measure of racial attitudes—important as they are, do not determine or reflect black attitude in all significant areas of life.

The chapter ends with an analysis of a puzzling non-monotonic relationship between the Alienation Index and a question on obedience to the law. The analysis reaffirms our sense of the index as a coherent and understandable measure, but also warns us not to forget the problems inherent in communication between research investigators and respondents.

7

CONCLUSIONS,
METHODOLOGICAL LIMITATIONS,
AND RECOMMENDATIONS

We can draw together the major findings of this analysis of black attitudes and attitude change between 1968 and 1971 with the following conclusions:

1. The two surveys that immediately preceded and followed the assassination in 1968 of Martin Luther King show no evidence of attitude change, militant or otherwise. The second of the two 1968 surveys suggests that the assassination was responded to by black Detroiters as a tragic human event which would, if anything, awaken whites to a better understanding of racial injustice, but that it probably did not immediately affect other black racial attitudes.

2. The evidence is quite strong that between 1968 and 1971 black attitudes did change. Although we are limited by the range and number of questions available, the most important shift seems to be in perceptions of whites. More blacks saw "most whites" as hostile and oppressive in 1971 than did in 1968. It is no surprise, therefore, that more blacks were also willing in 1971 to conceive of the need for extreme measures including violence to achieve their own rights. Very likely the perception of white hostility and the willingness to consider the need for strong black counter-measures go hand in hand in this situation. The one thing clear is that whatever may have happened to white attitudes since 1968, blacks have a less benign, though possibly more realistic, picture of whites now than at that earlier point.

3. Evidence for change in other areas is much less clear. One question on preference for black residential separation shows a significant but small increase, but two other questions dealing with separatist and black consciousness themes reveal no change at all. Beliefs about the pervasiveness of job discrimination have not changed significantly. And the increased suspicion of general white intentions does not seem to involve rejection of the country as a whole, if this is properly measured by willingness to fight for the United States in a major war. The pattern of black attitudinal change is far from total.

4. It is difficult to say whether the overall amount of change is "great" or "small," and of course impossible to know whether it is continuing at the rate detected here. Our eleven main questions show a shift of some six percentage points in three years, which is not trivial but also cannot be characterized as massive. It is also incorrect to view the black population as rapidly becoming of one mind in hostility toward whites, or indeed as monolithic on any other issue we surveyed. In fact, on most of the thirteen questions available in both 1968 and 1971, change tends to move the black population as a whole away from an essentially conservative stance and toward something like a fifty-fifty division. This apparent movement is at least partly a result of our own question wording, but not entirely, and the point deserves some note when talk centers too much on sweeping transformations of the total black population.

5. Although the eleven directional items asked in 1968 and repeated in 1971 constitute a rather miscellaneous set, they all intercorrelate positively at a low moderate level, with little change in the pattern or degree of association over the three-year period. So far as we can tell from this set of items, the *organization* of black attitudes did not shift noticeably between 1968 and 1971. Moreover, it makes sense to treat the items together in the form of a single index for much analysis, even though they also deserve (and receive) separate study.

6. We have labeled this eleven-item index "Alienation from White Society" on the basis of the content of the items. Later analysis of the correlates of the index supports such a conceptualization. High scores on the measure reflect a sense that neither individual whites (at the level of personal interaction), nor white-controlled organizations and institutions (at the community and societal levels), deserve to be trusted. Low scores can be seen to indicate the opposite, though our analysis has spoken less directly to this pole of the index. The distribution of scores is not bell-shaped, but rather skewed toward the high end. It seems theoretically possible that "middle scorers"—those who show some signs of alienation and militancy but not at an extreme level—are also distinctive. We found no evidence of this, but our analysis was not particularly well designed to detect such signs.

7. In carrying out analysis of the items, it is important to take account of race-of-interviewer as an independent variable. As demonstrated in several previous studies and replicated with our 1971 data, black respondents are more apt to give "anti-white" responses when the interviewer is black than white. The difference produced by race-of-interviewer tends to be greater than the change registered over the three years, hence the former could distort the latter if not attended to. (Age-of-interviewer, on the other hand, has little or no effect on responses.) Statistical control of interviewer effects should be straightforward, since there does not appear to be interaction between such effects and change over time: response levels change at about the same rate for both black and white interviewers. There is evidence, however, that education and race-of-interviewer do interact with respect to Alienation scores, and controls are needed in such analysis. There is also evidence that race-of-interviewer effects extend to political items that do not mention race explicitly, hence that they need control in political studies where racial issues are implicit rather than explicit variables.

8. The shift in attitudes that occurred between 1968 and 1971 appears to represent largely intra-individual change, rather than mainly the movement of younger people into adulthood and the passing of an older generation. The latter phenomena do account for part of the shift, but the greater part is attributed to alterations in the attitudes of those members of the same basic adult population surveyed in both years. At the same time, in 1971 as well as in 1968, age provides a major line of division within the black population: young adults (in our samples, ages 21-29) have sharply higher scores than older persons.[1]

---

[1]As noted at an early point, the Kerner-68 sample included persons 16-20, although we excluded them from all our main analysis because of their non-comparability in age to the two DAS samples. However, near the end of our analysis, we did keep in this younger age category for a single run. They turn out to be slightly *lower* in Alienation scores than persons 21-29, though higher than all other age categories. This unexpected result led us to look separately by age at each of the six index items available in the Kerner-68 survey. The 16-20 age category is lower in "alienation" than other age groups on the two items dealing with beliefs about whites (Keep Down and Trust) but higher (more alienated) on the remaining items. This may seem a puzzling result since the two items mentioned showed significant change between 1968 and 1971. In any case, we must leave this and some other puzzles in the data unresolved at this point. It is hoped that a replication of the Kerner-68 15-city survey will be carried out in the next few years, providing information relevant to this and several other remaining problems. For now we must simply note that the inverse relation of age to Alienation scores apparently levels off in 1968 below age 21.

9. Neither sex, education, nor family income give much evidence of interacting with time difference to produce distinctive patterns of change. But when the main 1968 and 1971 surveys are collapsed into a single larger data set, we do find evidence of interaction among age, education, and the Alienation Index: for younger persons only, high scores occur among the best and the least educated, while for older persons this U-shaped relationship disappears. Thus for those under age 35 (and to a lesser degree for the sample as a whole), Alienation is lowest for the middle educated groups and rises among *both* the most- and the least-educated.

10. Although the Alienation Index does not include direct measures of behavior, it is related to behaviors measured in the form of self-report. On the one hand, high scoring individuals report fewer friendly interactions with individual whites and more negative experience with white agents of control such as the police. At the same time, high scorers also tend to report more personal involvement in various forms of protest activities, although they do not report greater participation in such conventional political action as contributing to candidates and parties.

11. Alienation scores are significantly related to attitudes toward a variety of issues not explicitly racial, notably, personal income, religion, and government and public institutions, as well to a range of directly racial topics (see Chapter 6). Somewhat unexpectedly, those high in Alienation from White Society tend to score low on a measure of Personal Efficacy. This suggests a broad sensitivity on the part of high scorers to external as against internal obstacles to personal achievement. In this connection, it is well to note that aggregate change in black attitudes over time and variation at any given point within the black population are not necessarily due to the same factors.

12. Despite the wide range of other items and issues correlated with the Alienation Index, it is incorrect to assume that it is somehow connected to all areas of life. Beliefs about sex roles, to take one example, seem unrelated to position on the Index, and there are other important spheres described in the text which reveal little or no association to our measures of black racial attitudes.

Generality of Results

Much of our data came from a single city, Detroit, and there is a natural question about their generalizability to the country as a whole, or at least to other major urban areas. Indeed, in using the Kerner-68 full fifteen-city sample at points as well as the Detroit subset, we have assumed that these are interchangeable at least for purposes of drawing conclusions from correlational analysis.

We have no way of generalizing our data to the black population of the United States as a whole, and would certainly hesitate to leap from findings about Detroit or even the entire fifteen cities to, say, the black population in the rural Deep South. But we can report something about the relationship of our Detroit sample to that of the fourteen other cities included in the Kerner-68 survey. The Alienation Index (abb.) scores for all fifteen cities are presented in Table 29. Surprisingly, Detroit blacks show the *lowest* mean Alienation score for any of the fifteen cities, lower even than such Southern cities as Baltimore and St. Louis. (This finding in a different manifestation has been examined elsewhere [Schuman and Gruenberg, 1970: 244-247], with the conclusion being that it is not an artifact of sampling or other methodological problems.) While it would obviously be desirable to have a later replication comparing black attitudes in Detroit and other cities, for the present we must conclude that black Alienation in Detroit, at least in 1968, was noticeably lower than in the urban non-South generally. Of course, we cannot be sure that the difference of 1.8 points between mean scores for Detroit at the bottom of the listing and Milwaukee at the top is free of sampling error, but the gap of 0.8 points between Detroit and the mean (3.99) for the remaining fourteen cities is already larger than the 1968-1971 change for Detroit alone. Thus the shift over time must again be seen in the perspective of variation at one point in time.

TABLE 29

Mean Alienation Index Scores by City (Kerner-68)*

Milwaukee	4.97		Washington	3.98
Cincinnati	4.77		Cleveland	3.70
Brooklyn	4.67		San Francisco	3.70
St. Louis	4.26		Baltimore	3.59
Gary	4.25		Chicago	3.58
Newark	4.24		Philadelphia	3.43
Boston	4.08		Detroit	3.20
Pittsburgh	3.99			

*For the total table, d.f. $= 14, 2092$, F $= 6.89$, p $<.001$, E$^2 = 4.4\%$

More crucial to our analysis is the issue of whether relationships among variables are different in Detroit and the remaining fourteen cities. Since we are not for this purpose concerned with each of the fifteen cities separately, we compared a series of relationships for Detroit with those found in the fourteen remaining cities aggregated. Analysis of covariance was employed, with the Alienation Index treated as the dependent variable and Detroit vs. the combined 14 cities as the categorical variable. A series of measures from Chapter 6 were considered, one at a time, as interval-level independent variables:

> Belief that whites "dislike Negroes" (Table 20, No. 1)
> Belief that blacks have no chance to get ahead (Table 20, No. 2)
> Efficacy Index (Figure 5)
> Dissatisfaction with income (Table 26)
> Experiences with job discrimination (Table 25, No. 5)

In none of the five analyses could the hypothesis of equal slopes be rejected ($p > .25$ in all cases). It should also be recalled that in Chapter 5 when we looked at effects by age and the several socioeconomic status variables, relationships discovered for Detroit were generally replicated using the 15-city data.

Thus as far as we can tell, our inferences about *relationships* based on Detroit are generalizable to a combined set of 14 other major urban concentrations, and vice versa.[2] Beyond this we strongly suspect that our major results are generalizable to most urban black concentrations in the United States. We cannot show that the pace of change is the same elsewhere as in Detroit, and indeed it is sensible to expect it to vary with such local factors as leadership and history. Yet there seems little reason to doubt that the basic direction and approximate amount of change estimated in this study tell us a good deal about black attitudes and attitude change more broadly.

A Methodological Note on the Alienation Index

The items that compose our index of Alienation from White Society were chosen to maximize comparability among the three surveys drawn on

---

[2]This comparison of cities also provides a test of the effects of differences in response rate, since the Detroit response rate was quite high (88%) as compared with the average for the other 14 cities (74%).

for this report. We were not free to write new and better questions in 1971, nor even to select from the best items in either of the 1968 studies considered separately. Moreover, both conceptually and empirically the eleven Alienation items are obviously not measures of a single simple dimension. They do not all show similar change over time, nor in most other analyses do they all reveal identical associations with other variables. We have tried to handle this problem by carrying out much of our analysis at both the index and the item level, and thus to avoid simplistic assumptions of unidimensionality. For the most part broad conclusions are the same: the total index and the majority of the individual items behave similarly in our various analyses, even though it is rare for every item to follow the overall trend.

Where individual items do not perform the same way as the total index, they usually simply fail to show any association with the outside variable in question. Furthermore, having looked at many associations on both index and item level, we gradually have built up a sense that some of the index items are less "rich" than others in their correlations with a variety of non-index variables. Thus the question dealing with preferences for black neighborhoods (Table 1, No. 7) often shows a lower correlation than other index items with measures related to the overall index. Complexity of response seems at least part of the explanation: persons can choose a black (or white) neighborhood for several quite different reasons. For example, choice of a black neighborhood can be due to increased "black consciousness" in the current sense of allegiance to the black community, but it can also be due to a conservative preference for safe surroundings on the part of older Southern-born blacks. Likewise, it seemed possible that the Job item (Table 1, No. 5) is influenced by whether the respondent is in the labor market, and the Teacher item (No. 6) by whether there are school-age children in the family; preliminary analysis along these lines did not produce the expected interactions, but we continue to suspect that some such complexity of response may be a factor in their generally lower than average correlations with other variables. This single-item internal complexity is an undesirable feature of several of the index questions, and along with random response error contributes to the modesty of the interitem correlations reported in Chapter 3. Thus we do not by any means claim that all eleven items in the Alienation Index are as adequate as would be desirable.

Still the more important cause of the relatively low homogeneity of the index is probably the considerable diversity in both content and format of the eleven index items as a whole. From the standpoint of future trend studies, this diversity is as much a strength as a weakness, for it discourages too simple a picture of black attitudes and attitude change. Thus we would recommend repeating most of the eleven Alienation items in future studies of change. Where time is lacking for all eleven items, the abbreviated six-item Alienation set can be used. It is highly related to the full index (over .80 in both 1968 and 1971) and is somewhat more homogeneous in conceptual content, though it still includes both belief and action-oriented questions. Finally, we suggest that future trend research on black attitudes replicate the two items that head the list of racial correlates of the Index (Table 20). Dealing, respectively, with black beliefs about white attitudes toward blacks and with black assumptions about racial obstacles to success in America, the items refer to two of the most essential concerns of black Americans about their position in the larger American Society.

But just as we have worked with individual items as well as with the full index, future users should keep in mind that the relationships among these index items are not only small in size but problematic in conceptual terms. We do not claim to have identified a unique personality dimension, nor even a single attitude in terms of means or ends, but only a loosely organized set of beliefs, evaluations, and action orientations that fit together reasonabiy and empirically in the present period of American history. It is possible that a broad structural investigation of black attitudes could establish a more fundamental set of measures,[3] though many years of extensive work on white racial attitudes still leaves that parallel effort in an uncertain state. One such attempt for blacks (Marx, 1967) was outdated almost at the time of its publication (see Paige, 1970), and we suspect that in a period of rapid racial change it will be difficult to identify a stable but differentiated set of black racial attitudes. If such a new effort is undertaken, it would be well to have initial recourse to extensive open-ended questioning before attempting to devise a set of closed items for further analysis.

The Future

What of the future, not only beyond 1971 when our last survey was completed, or early 1974 when this monograph is being finished, but for at least the remaining years of the 1970's? Our own belief is that a sea-change occurred in black attitudes in the mid-60's, and that the urban riots which reached their peak in 1967 and 1968 were both an effect and a substantial further cause of this change. After the signs and symbols of progress

---

[3]Campbell and Schuman (1968) provide evidence for a distinction between purely cultural aspects of black consciousness and the more political emphasis on black separatism, but unfortunately the Alienation items are not really suitable for further testing of the validity of that distinction.

during the 1950's and early 1960's, the riots *crystallized* the belief among many blacks that progress was too slight and their status in American society still basically frustrating.[4] In one way, of course, the riots were simply a continuation of the black protest movements that had been gathering steam over the past decade, from the Montgomery bus boycott through the wide range of direct actions occurring in the early 60's. In another sense, the riots—and even more, the support they engendered in the black population (Campbell and Schuman, 1968, pp. 47-49, 55)— precipitated increased disillusionment with the more disciplined and optimistic earlier civil rights movement led by men like Martin Luther King.

This change in black views may well be as fundamental as the transformation in white views that began in the 1940's (if not before) and has been traced in a number of trend studies.[5] Whites began to become relatively more liberal in racial attitudes at that early date, and have continued this movement over the past three decades, though of course with a long way to go still from the black perspective. Now it appears that black views may have embarked upon an almost equally important shift and movement, one represented by the title of our main index, Alienation from White Society. Like white liberalism, moreover, the future potential of black alienation is indicated by the fact that it has its greatest hold on the young. There is good reason to speculate that in the years ahead both trends will continue: traditional white prejudice will decline further, but black disillusionment with whites will increase. If this seems paradoxical, it is perhaps no more so than the fact that black optimism survived so many long years of the most intense bigotry on the part of the majority of the white population.

The predominance of age as a correlate of black alienation probably reflects the strong ideological content of these changes in black attitudes. They represent a new way of seeing things and hence are adopted more easily by the young. At the same time, black alienation is a more complex phenomenon and has a wider mass base than does white liberalism. We have already seen that its association to education is not simple; unlike white liberalism, which tends to have higher schooling as a major and

---

[4]Political trend data from a series of Survey Research Center Election Studies presented by Miller, Brown, and Raine, 1973, are consistent with this interpretation of the point of major change.

[5]See the NORC studies by Sheatsley (1966), Schwartz (1967), and Greeley and Sheatsley (1971); the Survey Research Center trend data in Campbell (1971); and Detroit Area Study data in Duncan, Schuman, and Duncan (1973).

FIGURE 6a

Alienation Index Scores by Age (Kerner-68)

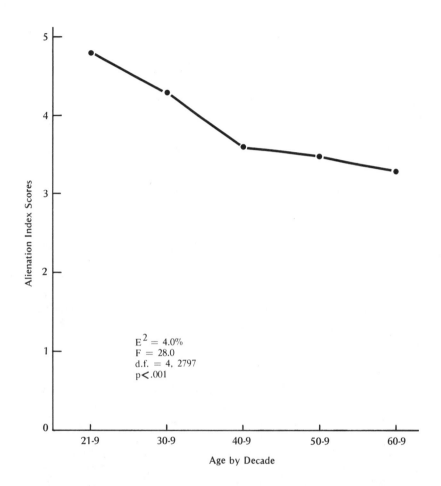

$$E^2 = 4.0\%$$
$$F = 28.0$$
$$d.f. = 4, 2797$$
$$p < .001$$

Age by Decade

monotonic correlate, black alienation clearly draws on sentiments held by the least educated as well as the most educated strata of the black population.

Moreover, even though the predominant source of rising alienation among blacks may be ideological, there are direct and continuing experiences and grievances feeding it which are not primarily ideological in character. This can be shown indirectly by comparing the relation of age to our heavily ideological index of Alienation with the relation of age to

FIGURE 6b

Reports of Hiring and Promotion Discrimination by Age (Kerner-68)

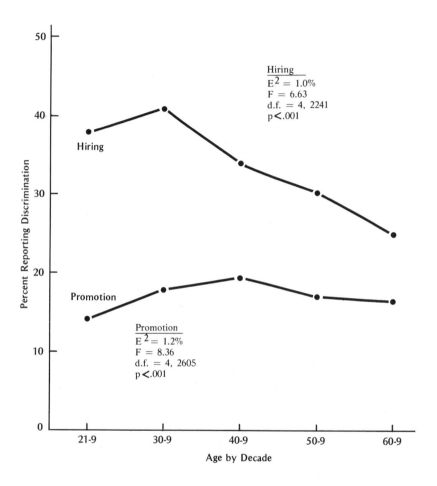

more direct reports of discrimination. The former relationship is shown in Figure 6-A, which is simply a picture (using Kerner-68 data) of associations already described in Chapter 5. The basic negative relationship of age to the Alienation Index is clear in the graph. Figure 6-B, however, reveals for this sample a different type of relationship between age and two measures of perceived discrimination: reports of hiring discrimination and of promotion discrimination reach their peak not among the young, but among those in their middle years. The most sensible interpretation of the curves is that they reflect the fact that the "opportunity to experience discrimination" is career-related,[6] and that it does not become strong until the working years of life. Indeed, one even notes that reports of discrimination in hiring peak at an earlier point than those for promotion, exactly as must be true for such experiences in real life. If we recall that these same grievances are positively related to the Alienation Index (see Table 25 above), we see that some of the sources of black Alienation involve personal experiences that are probably independent of the broad ideological changes described above.

In sum, the roots of black alienation are complex, to be found partly in general ideological and cultural change, as reflected in the much greater alienation of black youth, but partly in continuing racial experiences of a personal nature that are tied directly to position in the social structure. Indeed, our earlier results with the Efficacy Index suggested that personality factors contribute also. Thus black alienation in the 1970's is partly a reflection of overall group ideology, partly of roles and careers, and partly of individual attitude, as we have documented at various points in this report.

---

[6]This nicely ironic phrase appears in an unpublished working paper for DAS-68 by Jean Converse (1968).

APPENDIX A

EQUATING THE THREE SURVEYS: FURTHER DETAILS

Although each of the three samples dealt with in this volume can be described in general terms as a cross-section of the Detroit adult black population, each has special features which make a comparison with the other two samples imprecise without adjustments. These various features and adjustments are presented in Table A-1, and each is discussed below in the same order of presentation.

1. Geographic Area. Both Kerner-68 and DAS-68 drew black samples from the city of Detroit only, but DAS-71 drew blacks from the city and the surrounding suburbs (for an exact description of the DAS-71 geographic boundaries, see Fischer, 1972). Of all blacks aged 21 to 69 in DAS-71, 20 live outside Detroit. Since some black families probably moved from the city to the suburbs between 1968 and 1971, one might argue for widening the boundaries for the latter date, but in fact most of the black "suburban" population lives in stable self-contained towns bordering Detroit (including two enclaves). For simplicity, we have limited the DAS-71 sample to Detroit city only, thus making the boundaries identical to the two earlier studies.

2. Sex. In Kerner-68 and DAS-71, no special sampling restrictions were placed on sex of household members, and as occurs regularly in surveys (and the Census) we obtained a disproportionately large number of females. To increase the number of males (though of course not replacing those missed), DAS-68 systematically oversampled males. For comparison purposes in Table 1, we calculated all figures separately for each sex, then averaged the two in order to produce final figures on the assumption of equal weight for males and females. In most later tables where such

TABLE A-1 (*Sheet 1 of Table A-1*)

Special Features of the Three Detroit Samples that Require Control

	Original Kerner-68	Original DAS-68	Original DAS-71	Final Samples Unless Otherwise Specified
1. Geographic Area	Detroit City	Detroit City	Detroit City and suburbs	Detroit City
2. Sex Requirement	None	Males over-sampled to obtain 50%	None	(1) Sex weighted to 50/50 for all studies, or (2) Sex controlled by MCA
3. Eligible Ages	16 - 69	No lower limit - 69	21 - No upper limit	Ages 21 - 69 inclusive
4. Persons Eligible in Household	Any family member	Heads and wives of heads only	Any family member	Heads and wives of heads only

Footnotes are presented on Sheet 2 of this table.

TABLE A-1 *(Sheet 2 of Table A-1)*

	All black	Partly black and partly white on random basis, plus non-comparable portion inter-viewed by blacks	Partly black and partly white on random basis, but assignment ratios varied by integration of area	
5. Race of Interviewer				(1) Only blacks interviewed by blacks, with necessary weighting for DAS-68, or (2) Race of interviewer controlled by MCA
6. Other Weighting	Minor	Upper income areas over-sampled (by 2.0)	None	(1) For DAS-68, lower income areas weighted by 2.0, or (2) Income controlled using MCA
7. Response Rate	88%	83%	80%*	(No correction)
Original Unweighted N	199	619	406	
Final unweighted N for this analysis	148	600	384	

*Applies to total sample, including white respondents. Separate black rate not available.

weighting is not used, a statistical control for sex is included in MCA runs.

3. Eligible Ages. Since the eligible age ranges of the three samples differed somewhat, the common denominator is used throughout, namely, ages 21 to 69 inclusive.

4. Eligible Persons in Household. Both Kerner-68 and DAS-71 defined as eligible all persons in the primary family in the appropriate age range; but DAS-68 interviewed only heads and wives of heads of house,[1] excluding older children and other relatives living with the family. With the age range restricted to 21 to 69, the number of respondents who were not heads or wives of heads is small: 14 in Kerner-68, 24 in DAS-71.[2] For simplicity we have usually limited all three comparison samples to heads and wives, but in Chapter 5 we deal with non-heads and non-wives in the course of analysis and in Chapter 6 we note departures for DAS-71 from the general limitation to heads and wives.

5. Race of Interviewer. Kerner-68 used only black interviewers, but DAS-68 and DAS-71 each employed both black and white interviewers within a randomized design. As we discuss elsewhere in this volume, race-of-interviewer is an important variable in racial attitudes and requires attention throughout. Table 1 controls race-of-interviewer by limiting results to those interviewed by blacks only. Elsewhere statistical control is usually effected through MCA.[3] Regardless of the method, certain complications occur for each of the DAS years:

a) DAS-68. The original design for this study included a randomized "comparable" portion of 495 cases, exactly two-thirds (330) of whom were interviewed by blacks and one-third (165) by whites. Assignment of interviewers by race for these 495 cases was random. But the basic probability sample of Detroit also included 124 "non-comparable" cases arbitrarily assigned to black interviewers, as discussed in Schuman and Converse (1971).[4] All three parts of the sample are needed to represent the Detroit population, but this representation does not control for race-of-interviewer. Such control can be obtained in two ways. First, a representative

---

[1]Where the only adults in a household were husband and wife, the husband was arbitrarily designated as head. For a non-married person, with or without other family members, "head" was a matter of self-report.

[2]Two of the 24 DAS-71 cases also lived outside of Detroit.

[3]In Chapter 6 we generally dispense with race-of-interviewer as a control for reasons stated there.

[4]Table 1 of that article shows that the 124 cases are similar in age, sex, and education to the comparable portion, but appreciably lower in family income.

sample of Detroit can be constructed by weighting the 330 comparable cases interviewed by blacks by 1.5 (to compensate for the 165 cases omitted because they were interviewed by whites) and adding this sum to the 124 "non-comparable" cases. The final sample (unweighted N = 454, weighted N = 619) is representative of the entire Detroit black population and includes only cases interviewed by blacks. A second alternative is to include all 619 original cases regardless of race of interviewer, then control race-of-interviewer statistically during analysis. The first alternative is used in Table 1, the second at most later points.

It is not possible using DAS-68 to construct a precisely representative Detroit sample of blacks interviewed by *whites,* since the available respondents come from only the "comparable" portion of the black population, and we have no basis for estimating how the non-comparable portion of the black population would have answered questions put to them by white interviewers. However, to the extent that we are able to identify the main variables (e.g., income) which distinguish the comparable and non-comparable portions of the sample we can control for them statistically. Specifically, if we wish to compare responses to white interviewers in 1968 and 1971, we run MCA with Year as a predictor, along with such control predictors as income, and interpret the adjusted means as representing blacks-interviewed-by-whites freed of the differential effects of income for the two years. Since we cannot be sure that we have included all the relevant variables needed to equate the two samples (1968 and 1971), such results must be considered more tentative than when we deal with blacks interviewed by blacks and with the total sample.

b) DAS-71. Randomization of race-of-interviewer here was complete and approximates a simple model, but a minor qualification is needed. This resulted from our desire to randomize not only race-of-interviewer but also a cross-cutting distinction between interviewers provided by the Detroit Area Study, most of whom were young graduate students, and professional interviewers, mainly older, employed by the Survey Research Center. For details of these rather complicated but substantively not very significant variations, see Fischer (1972). The effect on the race-of-interviewer randomization is that the ratio of black interviewers to white interviewers differed somewhat for different "strata" of the city, where strata were determined by observation of percentage of households black during the field phase of sampling. The ratios were as follows:

Percentage of	Number of respondents interviewed			
segment black	By blacks	By whites	Total	Black/White
I. 0-15%	21	26	47	.81
II. 16-45%	15	11	26	1.36
III. 46-85%	23	29	52	.79
IV. 86-100%	173	85	258	2.04
	232	151	383	1.54

Within each stratum, race-of-interviewer was assigned randomly, but the ratio differs from one stratum to another. A series of test runs indicates that results based on taking account of strata (through weighting or MCA) differ only very slightly from results obtained if simple random assignment is assumed over the entire sample. This probably results from the fact that effects of the variations in ratios across the strata are slight, while in addition the bulk of the sample lies entirely within one stratum (IV). Because of the trivial effects of stratum, we have not attempted to control for it directly in our analyses; insofar as it is related to sex, SES, or other predictors used in MCA, it is controlled indirectly.

6. Other Special Problems. There are no further problems of design for DAS-71. The other two studies each have an additional special problem.

a) Kerner-68. In order to include younger blacks—of no relevance to the present comparison where 21 must be the lower age limit—two persons were sometimes interviewed in larger families. This was done within the framework of the basic probability sample, and indeed fits such a framework better than does the restriction of cases to one per household in the DAS and most other surveys. For the Kerner-68 Detroit sample, 28 of the 199 respondents interviewed came from the same households, that is, from 14 households (e.g., a father and also a daughter over 20 years of age). However, when only heads and wives are included in our Kerner-68 sample, the number of such pairs shrink from 16 to 7 (i.e., 14 respondents). We have not attempted to eliminate further this slight clustering within households. [5]

b) DAS-68. This survey double-sampled black households judged ahead of time to be above the median in value of housing, as a way of increasing the number of middle-class black respondents for certain analyses. To represent the black population correctly, it is necessary to compensate for this double-sampling of upper income households by

---

[5]There is also in Kerner-68 a weight to take account of a slight underrepresentation of blacks in largely white areas. Only seven cases would be so weighted (by 2.0) and the effect seems to be nil. We have not used that weight in these comparisons.

double-weighting lower income households (N=225). This has been done for Table 1, but in most later tables the problem is handled by including income as a predictor in MCA.

7. Response Rate. The response rates for the three studies vary from 88 percent to 80 percent. We have no direct information as to the effect, if any, of this variation, and do not attempt a correction. (However, see above p. 122).

8. Migration. Beyond the problems of equating the Detroit population in each survey by age, relation to head of house, and other defining variables, there is the possibility of change in any given population through selective migration and mortality. Since we deal only with a three-year period, this is assumed to be a minor problem for the present analysis and we have not attempted to deal directly with it.

A Final Note

The reader who has pursued the description of sample differences to this point may well wonder at the large number of variations among the three samples and at the difficulties of making exact comparisons across studies. Two points in this regard deserve emphasis. First, many of the differences have little effect, of any kind, as we show in the text at several points, and those that do have minor effects are probably well enough controlled so that they do not seriously distort findings. But second, these various differences do make comparisons somewhat more problematic, and serve to emphasize the need for cross-checking of conclusions. Although the nature of replication is somewhat different in social change studies than in the single cross-section investigation, the need is no less essential.

APPENDIX B

RANDOM PROBE RESPONSES
FOR SIX INDEX ITEMS

Open probe responses, as described on p. 25, were obtained for the six index items used in the Kerner-68 survey. These responses, as categorized by a project investigator, are shown below for each item. Where a given category subsumed many responses, only a representative selection is given. The frequencies shown are those for the subsample to whom the probe was addressed for each question.

1. Progress: *"Some people say that over the past 10 or 15 years, there has been a lot of progress in getting rid of racial discrimination. Others say that there hasn't been much real change for most (Negroes) over that time. Which do you agree with most?"*

        1. Lot of progress   36
        2. Not much real change   13
        8. Don't know   1

Lot of Progress
    (22) In Terms of Jobs, Housing, Education
"There are lots of places where Negroes now can work."
"People in all different states are getting more jobs. They are doing better than they ever have."
"Well, more jobs and better jobs have opened up for Negroes in the past 10 or 15 years. Negroes are being better educated. More of them are owning homes, traveling, doing things."
"Well, look at the jobs that have been opened up and the Negroes

who hold high jobs in the government. Schools have been integrated. Better Housing. Oh, a lot of things that I can't think of."
"In employment. Integration of churches. There are more Negro Catholics now."
"In housing, they have better opportunities. In jobs, in department stores."
"There has been some progress in housing, more jobs and better housing available for some. Training programs that have helped people improve themselves."

(2) *Things Better Due to Riots, Demonstrations, Pressure*
"Negroes hold higher jobs because opportunities are greater. Demonstrations have helped. Even the riots have helped."
"Because we have put the pressure where it belongs. We haven't gotten leaders, real leaders to help us."

(4) *Things Better But Changes Still Needed*
"Toward the younger generation, progress has been made. Some but not very much."
"There should have been more and better jobs, better housing. More money should have been put in our hands, better positions for our children."
"Government is showing more interest. It seems that the more willing Negroes have to assume more responsibility."

(6) *Things Generally Good*
"We have laws that protect the people. Many Negroes are now enjoying the fruits of a better income."
"They get more consideration and are getting better breaks."
"Many Negroes and whites associate together now where formerly they didn't. Many avenues of races getting together have increased in business and labor. Many city jobs now open, depending not on color but on ability. . ."
"Well they have more people working for the city of Gary. And they have Hatcher in office and that's progress."
"Now we can go in places to eat. Be served properly. Attend shows. I sit where there is an empty seat. You get in line and wait your turn for service. You are treated like human beings."

(1) "As a nurse, I have had no problems. For those that want change and progress, I know they can make it."
(1) "Don't know."

Not Much Real Change

(2) *General Discrimination and Prejudice Is the Same*

"On the whole the prejudice of people is still the same. They are just pretending today."

"There is still as much discrimination as ever."

(8) *In Jobs, Housing, Schools*

"The overall picture like housing and schools—there hasn't been much change."

"We can do the same job as the whites but get unequal pay. Education is different in white and colored schools."

"Well there's housing, jobs, etc. denied us. We bought this nice furniture, thought we were going to buy a house. When they found out we were Negroes they wouldn't sell it to us."

"You see a Negro here and there. We can't still live everywhere. The children still can't go to good schools. The more hell we raise the more we will get."

(2) *Things Changed But Not Enough*

"There are some changes. There are a good many of our people working in department stores and offices now."

"I will say that we have progressed more through the summer than ever before, but we are still behind."

Don't Know

(1) "Last 2 or 3 years they have hired Negroes in stores as clerks and in banks too. I don't know about the last 10 or 15 years."

2. Keep Down: *"On the whole, do you think most white people in (CITY) want to see (Negroes) get a better break, or do they want to keep (Negroes) down, or don't they care one way or the other?"*

1. Better break	16
2. Keep down	12
3. Don't care	16
8. Don't know	2

Better Break

(5) *Restatement*

"I think they care. They want us to have a better break."

"I guess they could probably want to see them get better. Can't get no worse."

"Some white people are true, at least, and want to see all people dealt with fairly."

(5) Better in Terms of Jobs

"The ones I know seem to want to help you get ahead. Help us get jobs."

"They are giving a little better jobs. They are changing things around."

"They are out to help you more than you are yourself. In every way they help you get ahead. For instance where I work at, the white people try to help you. They don't do anything to pull you down. You pull yourself down. They try to learn you and give you a job that you can learn something from."

(3) Positive Characteristics of Whites, e.g., Not Prejudiced

"Well, the few whites that I know, they all wanted the same that I wanted. They didn't seem not to want any colored friends."

"Some are not too prejudiced against Negroes."

"I have white friends who have given me compliments, encouragement and awards for my efforts in sports to keep going on."

(1) "Due to the fact that the Jewish people are a great percentage of the population, I'd say they are all for us. We wouldn't have gotten as far as we have if it wasn't for the Jew."

(1) "Well, after the riots I think they have realized how explosive things are right in their faces, and it gives them better security."

(1) "They would like to see us do better if it does not affect their status. You know they would like to see us do better if it just happened and took no skin off their nose."

Keep Down

(5) Fear, Insecurity

"Well, you have whites who are poor but have better conditions. As long as you keep Negroes down they can't rise because of it."

"They can rise financially, jobs and better schools. Well if you keep the Negro down, the whites can keep the best of everything."

"They don't like Negro bosses and Negroes in good positions. They're not used to it and resent it. It threatens their security."

"So many want to keep us down so we can't get their jobs and move into their houses."

(2) Hatred

"Because I think that they hate us just that bad."

"Hate, that's why they want to keep the Negro down. Whites, some of them really hate."

(2) Paternalistic Control

"The way they act. They consider you dumb. They do not think you are able to do anything on your own."

"Most want to keep you down so you have to come to them for help and then they won't give you none."

(1) "Well, most kind of believe in slavery stuff. I have had a few get on my back, where you are in a white area looking for a job. They start calling you names. Some tell you that they don't have jobs for Negroes."

(1) "They will not trade with the Negro like the Negroes trade with them."

(2) "That's the way the white man is doing all over—is trying to keep Negroes down. And I'll feel sorry for this city when the boys from the war that's been fighting come back and be treated wrong, the way the Negroes are treated now."

Don't Care

(3) Lack of Understanding of Problem

"People are beginning to think about the problem of the Negro. On the whole most people don't think about the problem."

"Well, this is the way they are. They don't care too much about Negroes. Most of them don't understand Negroes."

"It varies. Some really want to see them get better. Others want to keep them down. Most don't care because they have, if they are wealthy, no reason to come in contact with Negroes. So they don't care."

(2) Lack of Results or Solutions to Problems

"If they cared they could have corrected or solved more of the problem than they have."

"Just a few of them would like to see Negroes get a better break. But the way they have been running they sure don't care about Newark or the Negroes in it."

(*4*) *Whites Not Appreciative of Negro Advancement*
"White people, unless they have the same problem of poverty, are not interested. They feel we are competition for better things."
"A white person does not want a Negro to get a high position."
"If the Negro gets ahead most white people would not appreciate that."

(*4*) *Negroes No Threat*
"I can only speak of those I work with. They don't consider the Negro as a threat to them. Anyway that is what they say."
"They feel that all Negroes are the same and feel they don't care so they don't worry about them."
"They don't care as long as they don't get in their way."

(*1*) "Because most of the white people dislike Negroes."
(*1*) "The only ones favorable are the ones who own businesses and have money, other than that they just don't care."
(*1*) "Well, you know I'm black. So I'm around the white brothers more on my job."

3. Trust: *"Do you personally feel you can trust most white people, some white people, or none at all?"*
        1. Most   8
        2. Some   39
        3. None   5

Most

(*3*) *Race Has Nothing To Do With It* (*General Trust*)
"Oh, you can trust most people. I don't see any way race has anything to do with it."
"I have no trouble. There are bad and good in all race."
"Most white people you can trust. Those I have dealt with have certainly been fair."

(*5*) *Experience*
"Where I go to school I'm treated as any individual, not as a colored boy."
"Our neighbors are not trying to hurt us. Sometime its my own people. I have some whites I'd rather be with than Negroes."
"You can depend upon them. I think if we went into town and needed favors, we could get them. There are a good many Negroes

that feel that way too. Well, we depend upon them for our living to a certain extent. No, I think those are the best - we depend upon them for our living and favors."

Some

(12) Restatement

"There are just some you can talk to and some you can't."
"Some of any people cannot be trusted."
"Some people you can put more confidence in. You can't afford that for all."
"I just feel you can trust some of them. I have confidence in some."
"Some are really friendly and nice. Others are not. They dislike you on general principles."

(1) Duplicity

"Because he doesn't show you his true self. He acts one way with Negroes, another with whites."

(4) General Distrust of People

"I don't have any reason to completely trust them."
"You cannot trust people in general."
"Very few people you can really trust no matter who they are. I don't know enough white people to know."

(21) Positive

(4) Sympathy-Awareness of Negro Situation

"They have proved that they are aware of the Negro situation."
"There are some white people in sympathy with the Negro, but there are more that hate the Negro."
"There are some white people who are sincere and dedicated to the Negro's plight."

(7) Color Makes No Difference

"I haven't had anyone to do anything to hurt me. I have been encouraged by whites. But some people can't be trusted—not necessarily only whites."
"Color does not make any difference when it comes to trust. There is good and bad in all of us."
"Because any individual is an individual and a particular white could be just as trustworthy or untrustworthy as a particular Negro."
"Well, race doesn't matter. It's the particular person."

(6) Experience-Friendship

"Because I have some friends who are white."

"A friend is the only one I really trust."

(4) Economic Reasons

"Well some do give you credit. I guess that's because they figure you got a job to pay them."

"There are whites you can trust. Well, that depends upon the dealings you have with them. Nine out of ten you have to deal with, therefore he wants your money and you trust him."

"You can trust a white man more when he owes you money because he hates to owe a Negro so he'll pay. Just in money matters, that's it."

(1) Don't Know

"I don't know why I said that. I'm trying to be fair about it. That's all."

None

(1) Lack of Contact

"I've never had much dealing with them. I for one would rather not have contact no more than having to pass them on the street and that's all."

(1) General Distrust

"Because I didn't trust nobody at all - not anybody no matter what race."

(3) Duplicity of Whites

"Because historically they have lied. For a period of 100 years white men broke every treaty they ever signed with the Indians. No white man in this country has ever been executed for the murder of a Negro. There is no reason to believe that white folks are suddenly becoming moral and honest."

"I feel the same way they do. They don't trust the Negro so why should I trust them."

"Whites hate blacks. They don't tell the truth about things. They only want to use the black man."

4. Clerks: *"Do you think(Negro)customers who shop in the big down-*
town stores are treated as politely as white customers, or are
they treated less politely?"

1. As politely as whites   28
2. Less politely   18
8. Don't know   5

As Politely as Whites

(15) *Equivalent Restatements*

"From what I've seen both are treated equally."

"I have not lived in the city very long. But downtown I think the
stores are very fair."

"I have never had any trouble. I don't know about anybody else,
but I am treated politely."

"I don't do very much shopping in the big stores but from what I
hear they're pretty nice."

(7) *Economic Reasons*

"Those people are after money and they have no time for foolish-
ness."

"Treat the Negro better cause they think they can sell Negro the
most."

"Everytime I go down there they treat me okay. I give them what
they want. My money, that's what."

"Those big stores want your money and the more of us the better.
Their sales depend on all people. They want my money, so treat all
people alike."

Other Reasons

(1) "They are treated about the same as far as I can see. If they act
politely they will be treated likewise."

(1) "They all are treated the same. When you have a nasty sales-
person that person is nasty to all."

(1) "There are always some who deserve mistreatment but I've
never had any trouble."

(1) "It's funny, but they're treated just as polite as the whites. Not
that they want to do it."

(1) "It depends on what race is working in the stores. I think the
white clerks are more friendly."

Misunderstanding

(1) "They got colored working for them and I go to them."

Less Politely

(3) *Pass Over Negro to Serve White*

"The way they serve you. If a white customer is standing she will serve the white first and skip by you and serve the white first."

". . .they pass by me to wait on another white."

"For one thing, if you're waiting for service in one of the stores the clerk will always recognize the white person before they recognize you."

(5) *Spend More Time with Whites*

"More effort put forth to sell the white man where they don't care whether the Negroes buy or not."

"I have sensed it. It has happened to me. They just don't wait on you or leave you standing there."

"Because they are not treated as politely. They want the business but the salespeople don't take up as much time with Negroes."

(2) *Salesmen Are Suspicious of Negroes*

"Often you are looked at as though you are trying to steal something."

"Most treat Negroes less politely because they feel Negroes don't have the money to spend or even know that they are looking for. They think Negroes are always going to steal something."

(7) *Treatment Differs: Other*

"Some cases Negroes are treated politely. But not always, so I'll buy half of the time less politely."

"I cannot quite analyse it, but my money spends just as good."

"When you walk into the stores the clerks become very courteous instead of letting you look around."

"They seem to be more courteous to the white people and they are nice to you too."

"It is according to your dress. A Negro is dressed . . . appealing to one's eye, you are treated nicely. But if dressed sloppy you are treated less politely."

"They don't always smile and thank you."

Don't Know

"All I shop at treat me fairly."

"I think Negro clerks in stores are less courteous in many instances than white clerks."

"I feel both races are treated about the same."

"I don't go to any stores here in D.C. I do all of my shopping in the Virginia stores where my home is."

"Depends solely on the clerk that is waiting on you. Although the store owners may demand respect and politeness, often their employees are prejudiced. Either the customer protests or leaves without purchasing."

7. **Best Means:** *"As you see it, what's the best way for (Negroes) to try to gain their rights — use laws and persuasion, use non-violent protest, or be ready to use violence."*
   1. Laws and persuasion   12
   2. Non-violent protest   19
   3. Violence if necessary   11
   7. Other (specify)   3
   8. Don't know   2

Laws and Persuasion

   (3) Restatement

   "Laws as are is a slow process but it's the best way to get their rights."

   "Because the laws are made to follow and through them with persuasion it would gain them their rights."

   "I don't know really but go to the law with your problems and see if they will help you. That's the best way."

   (3) Positive Power of the Law

   "Most people will obey laws and do as they are told."

   "If they have laws they might not break them if they have to pay a fine."

   "If Negroes unite, they can bring enough pressure that they can get rights through the courts. If it is not upheld in the courts, the U.S. is in for a sad awakening."

   (3) Anti-Violence

   "You should not fight for better rights. If you want to move up, you move up."

   "The more we prove we're law abiding the better things will be. We will be more respected. There will be less fear."

   (1) "Use God's Laws"

Non-Violent Protest

(3) Restatement

"Non-violence protests would make it easier for the Negroes."

"I was a picket to get jobs in a store down south and I think this works the best."

"Well non-violence protests is going and seeing about these problems and taking these things out in a peaceful and manageable way."

(7) Against Violence in General

"By knowing what the protest is about and a strong objective and I feel you can accomplish more by not using violence."

"Because it's never good when there is violence."

"Well I don't believe violence is necessary. Well I said that because Martin Luther King used it (non-violence) and it did some good."

(5) Consequences of Violence

"I don't believe in violence and when it happens it only causes people to get hurt or killed. That's why I believe in non-violent protests."

"I think the law or non-violence is alright. I know they won't get anywhere using violence. Violence won't do anything but get you killed. I don't believe in using violence."

"Violence is not going to help them. All violence will get them is jail."

Violence If Necessary

(1) Violence Without Loss of Life

"Talking didn't get them nowhere. Violence, if possible without loss of life."

(6) Violence Necessary: No Other Way

"Waiting for rights hasn't gotten these rights. Maybe it's not right but there's no other way."

"For 100 years we have been waiting and praying. Non-violence didn't get it. I think violent protest got more and we're going to have to use violence."

"Because the white man will not listen to nothing else."

"I don't think they can get by without it."

"They've been singing and praying all their lives. It will have to be violence I do believe."

(4) Violence Only as Last Resort

"Only when necessary use violence. Pray and wait on God."

"Really I think all three are important. It seems though that more attention is brought about by violence. So if that is what it takes I guess it will have to be that way."

"So far the Negro has not gotten no place when not using violence. So I would say, violence if necessary."

"Maybe the white people will listen to what they have to say, to let them have their rights, like if they want to move into a white section. If they don't, let them be ready to use violence."

Other

"Through *education* they will get the necessary knowledge for improving themselves."

"This is where your *vote* counts. Votes are important."

"*Nothing.* Quit fighting. What good is that non-violence drilling. What good is that. I am doing all right by not fighting. I take the job I can get."

Don't Know

"I don't know how to answer that one."

"It's too hard to tell which is better."

9. Neighborhood: The following probe to the closed question was asked of all respondents except those who said "makes no difference": *"Why do you feel that way?"* Below are the open categories constructed on the basis of an extensive review of over a hundred completed interviews. Parenthesized figures are percentages based on the sample N of 2809.

(Negro) Neighborhood

(6.2%) 01. *More "comfortable" with Negroes; get along/understand each other better:* get along better with your own; don't feel welcome/comfortable with whites; I prefer the company of my own; have more fun.

(1.4%) 02. *(Mutual) incompatibility:* whites and Negroes don't get along; they don't want me and I don't want them; Negroes should live with Negroes and whites with whites.

(1.2%) 03. *Hostile and/or extreme reaction from whites:* would be afraid of being stoned in white neighborhood; whites threaten to call the city if you don't keep your yard clean; if you move into a white neighborhood, they will move out anyway.

(0.7%) 04. *Hostile and/or extreme reaction toward whites, or both ways:* I don't like whites; there would be conflicts and trouble.

White or Mixed Neighborhood

(17.7%) 05. *Lessen prejudice/get along/learn about/come to understand each other (n.e.c., see code 06):* we should learn to live together/have a better understanding of each other; if they live together they can find out what the other is really like; important for kids to know there are other people; if we live together it will erase the problem between races.

(8.7%) 06. *Race should not be relevant:* We are all human beings; one race is as good as another; Negroes should have the same feelings toward whites as they have toward other people; I can be friends with anybody; people should be able to live where they want; I'm against segregation.

(10.5%) 07. *Better neighborhood/higher standards:* Neater/cleaner; quieter; less crime, better neighborhood (unspecified).

(4.8%) 08. *Better services:* Schools, police protection; they'd have to give you the same service they give the whites; stores are stocked better.

Negro, White or Mixed

(2.9%) 09. *Traditional; familarity:* I have always lived in Negro/white/mixed neighborhood.

(1.4%) 10. Other.

(6.6%) 11. Don't know (includes, "I'd just like it," "All one way is no good.").

(37.9%) 00. Inapplicable; respondent answered "makes no difference," don't know, or N.A. on closed question.

REFERENCES

Allport, Gordon W.
1958 *The Nature of Prejudice.* Garden City, New York: Doubleday Anchor.
Blumenthal, Monica D., Robert L. Kahn, Frank M. Andrews, and Kendra B. Head
1972 *Justifying Violence: Attitudes of American Men.* Ann Arbor: The Institute for Social Research, The University of Michigan.
Bradburn, Norman M., and William M. Mason
1964 "The effect of question order on responses." *Journal of Marketing Research* 1:57-61.
Campbell, Angus, and Howard Schuman
1968 "Racial attitudes in fifteen American cities." In *Supplemental Studies for the National Advisory Commission on Civil Disorders.* Washington, D.C.: U.S. Government Printing Office, July, 1-67; New York: Frederick A Praeger, Publishers, 1-67; reprinted as a separate monograph by the Institute for Social Research, The University of Michigan, Ann Arbor.
Campbell, Angus
1971 *White Attitudes Toward Black People.* Ann Arbor: The Institute for Social Research, The University of Michigan.
Caplan, Nathan S., and Jeffery M. Paige
1968 "A study of ghetto rioters." *Scientific American* 219:15-21.
Caplan, Nathan S.
1970 "The new ghetto man: a review of recent empirical studies." *Journal of Social Issues* 26:59-73.
Carr, L.G.
1971 "The Srole items and acquiescence." *American Sociological Review* 36:287-293.
Converse, Philip E.
1964 "The nature of belief systems in mass publics." Pp. 206-61 in David E. Apter (ed.), *Ideology and Discontent.* New York: Free Press.
Crain, Robert L. and Carol Sachs Weisman
1972 *Discrimination, Personality and Achievement.* New York: Seminar Press.
Crawford, Thomas J., and Murray Naditch
1970 "Relative deprivation, powerlessness, and militancy: the psychology of social protest." *Psychiatry* 33:208-223.

Daniel, Johnnie
    1972   *Social Class Identification Among Blacks and Whites.* Unpublished Ph.D. dissertation, Department of Sociology, The University of Michigan.
Davis, James
    1974   "The Goodman system for significance tests in multivariate contingency tables." Pp. 189-231 in Herbert Costner (ed.), *Sociological Methodology 1973-74.* San Francisco: Jossey-Bass.
Duncan, Otis Dudley
    1967   "Discrimination against Negroes." *The Annals of the American Academy of Political and Social Science* 371:85-103.
Duncan, Otis Dudley, Howard Schuman, and Beverly Duncan
    1973   *Social Change in a Metropolitan Community.* New York: Russell Sage Foundation.
Edwards, Ozzie
    1972   "Intergenerational variation in racial attitudes." *Sociology and Social Research.* 57:22-31.
Edwards, Ozzie
    1973   "Skin color as a variable in racial attitudes of black urbanites." *Journal of Black Studies* 3:473-483.
Farley, Reynolds and Albert Hermalin
    1972   "The 1960s: a decade of progress for blacks?" *Demography* 9:353-370.
Fields, James M.
    1970-71   "The sample cluster: a neglected source of data." *Public Opinion Quarterly* 34:593-603.
Fischer, Elizabeth M.
    1972   "Sampling report for the 1971 Detroit Area Study." Ann Arbor: Detroit Area Study, The University of Michigan.
Ford, W. Scott
    1973   "Interracial public housing in a border city: another look at the contact hypothesis." *American Journal of Sociology* 78:1426-1447.
Forward, John R., and Jay R. Williams
    1970   "Internal-external control and black militancy." *Journal of Social Issues* 26:75-92.
Greeley, Andrew M., and Paul B. Sheatsley
    1971   "Attitudes toward racial integration." *Scientific American* 225:13-19.
Gurin, Patricia, Gerald Gurin, Rosina C. Leo, and Muriel Beattie
    1969   "Internal-external control in the motivational dynamics of Negro youth." *Journal of Social Issues* 25:29-53.
Gurin, Patricia, and Edgar Epps
    1974   *Achievement and Identity,* New York: Wiley (forthcoming).
Hannertz, Ulf
    1969   *Soulside.* New York: Columbia University Press.
Hatchett, Shirley, and Howard Schuman
    1974   The Effects of Black and White Interviewers on White Responses. Unpublished paper.
Huessenstamm, F.K.
    1971   "Bumper stickers and the cops." *Transaction* 8:32-33.
House, James S.
    1968   "Sampling report for the 1968 Detroit Area Study." Ann Arbor: Detroit Area Study, The University of Michigan.

Hyman, Herbert H.
  1954 *Interviewing in Social Research.* Chicago: University of Chicago Press.
Lenski, Gerhard E., and John C. Leggett
  1960 "Caste, class, and deference in the research interview." *American Journal of Sociology* 65:463-467.
Levine, Robert A., and Donald T. Campbell
  1972 *Ethnocentrism: Theories of Conflict, Ethnic Attitudes, and Group Behavior.* New York: Wiley.
Marx, Gary T.
  1967 *Protest and Prejudice.* New York: Harper and Row.
Meyer, Philip
  1969 "Aftermath of martyrdom: Negro militancy and Martin Luther King." *Public Opinion Quarterly* 33:160-173.
Miller, Arthur H., Thad A. Brown and Alden S. Raine
  1973 "Social conflict and political estrangement, 1958-1972." Paper presented at Midwest Political Science Association Convention, Chicago.
Murphy, Raymond and James M. Watson
  1970 "The structure of discontent: the relationship between social structure, grievance, and riot support." Pp. 140-257 in Nathan Cohen (ed.), *The Los Angeles Riots: A Socio-Psychological Study.* New York: Praeger.
Myrdal, Gunnar
  1964 *An American Dilemma.* New York: McGraw-Hill Paperback Edition.
Paige, Jeffery M.
  1970 "Changing patterns of anti-white attitudes among blacks." *Journal of Social Issues* 26:69-86.
Quarm, Daisy
  1971 "Do Black Interviewer Effects Exist?" Unpublished paper. Ann Arbor: Detroit Area Study, The University of Michigan.
Rotter, J.B.
  1966 "Generalized expectancies for internal versus external control of reinforcement." *Psychological Monographs* 80:1-28.
Schuman, Howard
  1966 "The random probe: a technique for evaluating the validity of closed questions." *American Sociological Review* 21:218-222.
Schuman, Howard
  1972a "Attitudes vs. actions *versus* attitudes vs. attitudes." *Public Opinion Quarterly* 36: 347-354.
Schuman, Howard
  1972b "Race relations: some policy implications, proximate and remote, of a negative finding." Paper prepared for the Carmel Conference, American Sociological Association.
Schuman, Howard
  1972c "Two sources of antiwar sentiment in America." *American Journal of Sociology* 78:513-536.
Schuman, Howard, and Barry Gruenberg
  1970 "The impact of city on racial attitudes." *American Journal of Sociology* 76:213-261.
Schuman, Howard, and Jean M. Converse
  1971 "The effect of black and white interviewers on black responses." *Public Opinion Quarterly* 35:44-68.

Schuman, Howard, and Otis Dudley Duncan
    1974   "Questions about attitude survey questions." Pp. 232-251 in Herbert
            Costner (ed.), *Sociological Methodology,* 1973-74. San Francisco: Jossey-
            Bass.
Schwartz, Mildred A.
    1967   *Trends in White Attitudes Toward Negroes.* Chicago: National Opinion
            Research Center.
Sheatsley, Paul B.
    1966   "White attitudes toward the Negro." *Daedalus* 95:217-238.
Supplemental Studies for the National Advisory Commission on Civil Disorders.
    1968   Washington, D.C.: U.S. Government Printing Office.
Thomas, W. I., and Dorothy Thomas
    1928   *The Child in America.* New York: Knopf.
Williams, J. A., Jr.
    1964   "Interviewer-respondent interaction: a study of bias in the information
            interview." *Sociometry* 27:338-352.
Williams, Robin M., Jr.
    1964   *Stranger Next Door.* Englewood Cliffs, New Jersey: Prentice-Hall.

INDEX